KETO DIET
COOKBOOK FOR BEGINNERS

140+ Core Recipes and a Week-by-Week Meal Plan to Boost Energy and Support Wellness. The Ultimate Guide to Health and Vitality with Low-Carb Nutrition

Copyright © 2024 by Maya Boles

All rights reserved. No part of this publication may be reproduced, distributed, or transmitted in any form or by any means, including photocopying, recording, or other electronic or mechanical methods, without the prior written permission of the author, except in the case of brief quotations embodied in critical reviews and certain other non-commercial uses permitted by copyright law.

This book is a work of the author's experience and research. While the author has made every effort to ensure the accuracy and completeness of the information contained in this book, the author assumes no responsibility for errors or omissions. The advice and recipes provided are not intended to be a substitute for medical advice or treatment. Please consult with a healthcare provider before making any significant changes to your diet or exercise program, especially if you have existing health conditions. The nutritional information provided in this book is based on the author's best estimates and should be treated as such. Individual results may vary.

Table of Contents

1 The Benefits of the Keto Diet
Introduction, p.4
What is Keto and How Does it Work? p.5
Introduction to Keto and Ketosis
Health Benefits of the Keto, p.5
Evidence-Based Health Benefits of the Keto Diet, p.5
Cultural Background of the Keto Diet, p.5
Mental and Emotional Benefits, p.6
Real-Life Success Stories, p.6
Practical Tips for Initial Success, p.6
Dealing with the Keto Flu, p.6
Incorporating Exercise into Your Keto Lifestyle, p.6
How to Use This Book, p.6

2 Getting Started on Keto
Essential Keto Pantry Staples, p.7
Keto-Friendly Kitchen Tools, p.7
Meal Planning and Prep Tips for Success, p.7
What to Eat and What Not to Eat on the Keto, p.8
Keto-Friendly Substitutions, p.8

3 Core Keto Recipes for Every Meal
Breakfast Recipes to Energize Your Mornings, p.10
Lunch Recipes to Keep You Going, p.20
Dinner Recipes to End Your Day Right, p.31
Snacks and Appetizers: Keep Your Energy Up, p.42
Desserts: Indulge Without Guilt, p.53

4 Unique Recipe Categories
Quick Weekday Meals, p.63
Weekend Feasts, p.67
Meal-Prep Friendly Recipes, p.70
Keto on a Budget, p.73
Keto for Families, p.74
International Keto Recipes, p.75
Holiday Recipes, p.76

5 Week-by-Week Flexible Meal Plan and Customization Guide
Week 1: Simple Keto Recipes to Get You Started, p.80
Customization Tips and Shopping List by Food Group for Week 1, p.81
Week 2: Exploring New Flavors and Ingredients, p.82
Customization Tips and Shopping List by Food Group for Week 2, p.83
Week 3: Energizing and Nutritious Meals, p.84
Customization Tips and Shopping List by Food Group for Week 3, p.85
Week 4: Staying Consistent and Satisfied, p.86
Customization Tips and Shopping List by Food Group for Week 4, p.87
Steps to Building Your Plan and Key Strategies for Customization, p.88
Weekly Customization Examples, p.88

6 Staying on Track – Challenges and Long-Term Success, p.89
Building a Long-Term Mindset
Advanced Tips for Overcoming Challenges
Cravings for Carbs
Weight Loss Plateaus
Social Situations and Dining Out
Incorporating Exercise for Long-Term Health
Transitioning to Maintenance

7 Real-Life Transformations Inspiring Success Stories, p.90

8 Keto Resources and Tools
Recommended Keto Books, Blogs, and Podcasts, p.91
Helpful Apps and Tools for Meal Planning, p.91
and Tracking Online Support Communities, p.91
Final Thoughts, p.92
Glossary of Keto Terms, p.93
Measurement Conversion Charts, p.93
Recipe Index by Meal Type, p.94

Introduction

Hi, I'm Maya Boles, and I'm thrilled to share this journey with you. For years, I struggled with weight issues, digestive discomfort, mood imbalances, and skin challenges. Sleepless nights and low energy were a constant, leaving me in a relentless pursuit of better health. When I discovered the ketogenic diet, everything changed. Not only did I reshape my body, but I finally found the energy, clarity, and a sense of wellness I'd been searching for.

My own journey with keto has been transformative, and it's my passion to help others experience that same change. Through this book, I've gathered over 140 simple, delicious recipes designed with beginners in mind, a flexible meal plan to guide you week-by-week, and practical tips to make keto both enjoyable and sustainable.

I've also had the joy of organizing a keto cooking group where we share tips, recipes, and encouragement. This community has deepened my commitment to helping others find success with keto, and I bring that same dedication to these pages. My hope is that this book inspires you, empowers you, and serves as a trusted guide on your own path to health and vitality.

Here's to finding joy, balance, and lasting success on the keto path!

The Benefits of the Keto Diet

What is Keto and How Does it Work?

The ketogenic diet, or keto for short, is more than just a weight-loss method—it's a lifestyle approach to achieving sustainable health, energy, and mental clarity. By dramatically reducing carbohydrate intake and focusing on healthy fats, your body enters a metabolic state called ketosis, where it burns fat for energy instead of relying on glucose from carbs. This shift can lead to transformative changes in physical and mental well-being.

Introduction to Keto and Ketosis

Ketosis occurs when the body's primary fuel source shifts from carbohydrates to fats. By reducing carbs and increasing healthy fats, you encourage your body to enter this fat-burning state, which can help with weight management, consistent energy levels, and overall metabolic health.

Unlike traditional diets that rely on calorie restriction, keto works by changing the source of energy your body uses, leading to lasting results. However, achieving ketosis can take a few days, depending on your body's metabolism and the types of foods you eat. Patience is essential during this adjustment period as your body learns to rely on fat for fuel.

Health Benefits of Keto

The keto diet offers several powerful health benefits:

- ✓ **Weight Loss and Fat Loss:** By burning fat for fuel, keto can help reduce body weight and target stubborn fat stores.
- ✓ **Improved Blood Sugar and Insulin Levels:** Limiting carbs stabilizes blood sugar, making keto especially beneficial for people with insulin resistance or type 2 diabetes.
- ✓ **Heart Health:** Healthy fats like those from olive oil and fatty fish can improve cholesterol levels, increasing HDL (good cholesterol) while reducing LDL (bad cholesterol) and triglycerides.
- ✓ **Reduced Inflammation:** Many keto-friendly foods have anti-inflammatory properties, which may help decrease the risk of chronic diseases.
- ✓ **Consistent Energy:** Unlike carb-heavy diets that lead to blood sugar spikes and crashes, keto offers a steady fuel source for the body and brain.

Evidence-Based Health Benefits of the Keto Diet

Several scientific studies have supported the benefits of the Keto diet, especially in relation to weight loss, metabolic health, and disease prevention:

A 2013 study published in the *British Journal of Nutrition* found that individuals following a ketogenic diet lost more weight and body fat than those following a low-fat diet. Participants on keto also showed significant improvements in triglyceride and cholesterol levels.

A 2018 review in *The European Journal of Clinical Nutrition* concluded that the ketogenic diet could improve insulin sensitivity, making it an effective approach for managing type 2 diabetes and reducing the risk of heart disease.

Research has also shown the potential of the Keto diet in neurological health. A study in the *Journal of Clinical Neurology* found that the diet has neuroprotective effects, which may help reduce the risk of conditions like Alzheimer's disease and epilepsy.

70-80% of daily caloric intake, focusing on **Healthy Fats** from sources like avocados, nuts, seeds, olive oil, fatty fish, and coconut oil.

Proteins:
15-20%, derived from high-quality meats, poultry, eggs, and dairy products.

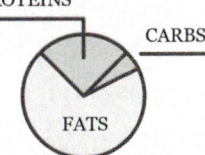

Carbohydrates:
5-10%, mainly coming from non-starchy vegetables such as spinach, broccoli, and cauliflower.

Cultural Background of the Keto Diet

The ketogenic diet originally emerged in the 1920s as a medical treatment for epilepsy, helping to reduce seizures in patients by altering their metabolism. While its therapeutic roots are still recognized today, keto has evolved into a popular lifestyle choice for people looking to improve their metabolic health, manage weight, and increase energy.

Similar to low-carb traditional diets in Mediterranean and indigenous cultures, keto emphasizes natural, whole foods and healthy fats—principles that have long been associated with long-lasting health.

Mental and Emotional Benefits of Keto

Beyond physical benefits, many people experience improvements in mental clarity and emotional stability on keto:

- ✓ **Steady Focus and Mental Clarity:** Ketones provide a stable and efficient energy source for the brain, reducing "brain fog" and improving concentration.
- ✓ **Mood Stability:** Stable blood sugar levels help avoid the energy crashes that often lead to mood swings.
- ✓ **Better Sleep and Reduced Anxiety:** Many keto followers report improved sleep quality and a more balanced emotional outlook.

Real-Life Success Stories

Keto has transformed the lives of countless individuals. Here are two brief success stories to inspire you on your journey:

> *Emily, 42: Keto helped me lose the weight I had struggled with for years. But more importantly, I felt energized, focused, and healthier than ever.*
>
> *James, 35: After trying several diets, keto finally gave me the energy and mental clarity I was looking for. My afternoon energy crashes disappeared, and I felt more productive than ever.*

These stories highlight how keto's impact extends beyond physical transformation, enhancing quality of life.

Practical Tips for Initial Success

Starting keto can present challenges, but a few strategies can ease the transition:

Managing Keto Flu: Some people experience temporary symptoms, like fatigue or headaches, as their bodies adapt to burning fat instead of carbs. Combat this by drinking plenty of water, balancing electrolytes with foods like avocados and leafy greens, and gradually increasing fat intake.

Simple Food Swaps: Replace carb-heavy foods with keto-friendly alternatives. Try lettuce wraps instead of bread, zucchini noodles for pasta, and cauliflower rice in place of regular rice.

Dining Out on Keto: Opt for grilled meats, salads, and vegetables, and don't be afraid to ask for substitutions. Many restaurants are happy to accommodate low-carb requests.

Incorporating Exercise into Your Keto Lifestyle

Exercise complements keto by enhancing both physical and mental benefits:

- ✓ **Strength Training:** Supports muscle preservation and increases metabolism.
- ✓ **Cardio Workouts:** Enhances fat burning and improves heart health.
- ✓ **Flexibility and Recovery:** Yoga and stretching support balance and recovery, promoting long-term health.

Exercise, when combined with keto, can elevate your health results, supporting both weight loss and energy maintenance.

How to Use This Book?

This book is designed to guide you step-by-step through your keto journey:

Start with the Basics: Chapter 1 covers the benefits of the Keto diet, helping you understand how it works.

Get Prepared: In Chapter 2, "Getting Started on Keto," you'll find guidance on setting up a Keto-friendly kitchen, pantry staples and essential kitchen tools. This chapter also offers practical meal planning and prepping tips.

Core Keto Recipes for Every Meal: Chapter 3 contains 100+ carefully selected recipes for breakfast, lunch, dinner, snacks, and desserts.

Unique Recipe Categories allows you to explore new flavors, experiment with cooking styles, and further customize your Keto experience.

Holiday Feasts and Celebration Recipes: For a special touch, you'll find a bonus section with holiday-inspired recipes, perfect for Thanksgiving, Christmas, and other festive gatherings. These recipes allow you to stay Keto-friendly even during special occasions.

Flexible Week-by-Week Meal Plan will guide you through your first month on Keto, making it simple to stay consistent and on track. This chapter includes weekly shopping lists, meal prep tips, and a customizable structure so you can adjust your plan to fit your lifestyle and preferences.

Overcoming Challenges and Keto Resources sections provide motivation, practical advice, and additional tools for making keto sustainable long-term.

Getting Started on Keto

Starting a Keto lifestyle is exciting but can seem overwhelming at first. This chapter is designed to set you up for success by preparing your kitchen, stocking essential ingredients, and developing effective meal planning habits. With the right staples and tools, and a little planning, you'll be ready to embrace Keto with ease and confidence.

Essential Keto Pantry Staples

Building a Keto-friendly pantry is all about choosing foods that are high in healthy fats, moderate in protein, and low in carbs. Here's a list of must-have ingredients to help you create satisfying, Keto-friendly meals:

Healthy Fats: Coconut oil, olive oil, ghee, butter, and avocado oil are excellent for cooking and salad dressings.

Low-Carb Vegetables: Stock up on leafy greens (spinach, kale), cruciferous vegetables (broccoli, cauliflower), zucchini, and bell peppers.

Protein Sources: Choose high-quality meats like grass-fed beef, chicken, and fatty fish (salmon, mackerel). Eggs are also a versatile, nutrient-rich option.

Nuts and Seeds: Almonds, walnuts, chia seeds, and flaxseeds are great for adding healthy fats and fiber.

Dairy and Non-Dairy Alternatives: Hard cheeses, heavy cream, and unsweetened almond milk add creaminess and richness.

Keto-Friendly Sweeteners: Use sugar substitutes like stevia, erythritol, or monk fruit for baking or adding a touch of sweetness without carbs.

Herbs and Spices: Flavor your dishes without carbs by incorporating herbs and spices like basil, rosemary, turmeric, and garlic powder.

These ingredients are the foundation of many Keto recipes and will help you easily transition into a low-carb, high-fat diet.

Keto-Friendly Kitchen Tools

Here are some tools that simplify Keto cooking and allow you to get creative with your meals:

Spiralizer: Perfect for making "zoodles" or spiralized vegetables as a pasta substitute.

Food Processor: Useful for making cauliflower rice, keto-friendly sauces, and dips.

Air Fryer: This tool allows you to make crispy, fried foods without excess oil.

Blender: Essential for smoothies, bulletproof coffee, and blending sauces or soups.

Digital Food Scale: Helps you accurately measure portions, especially when tracking macronutrients (macros).

Storage Containers: Invest in quality, air-tight containers for meal prepping and storing leftovers.

Meal Planning and Prep Tips for Success

Plan Your Weekly Menu: Start by choosing recipes for breakfast, lunch, dinner, and snacks for the week. Refer to the 30-Day Keto Meal Plan for ideas and customize based on your preferences.

Batch Cooking: Prepare large portions of Keto staples like grilled chicken, hard-boiled eggs, and cauliflower rice. These can be used in meals throughout the week.

Organize Ingredients by Meal: Portion out ingredients for each meal in advance, storing them in labeled containers. This saves time and reduces stress during busy weekdays.

Make Use of Leftovers: Incorporate leftovers creatively in different dishes. For instance, leftover grilled chicken can be added to salads or wraps.

Stay Flexible: Having a plan is important, but allow room for flexibility. Swap meals within the week if your schedule changes or you're craving something different.

These steps will keep you organized, make cooking more efficient, and ensure you're always ready to enjoy delicious, Keto-friendly meals.

Measurement	Equivalent
Teaspoons (tsp)	1 tsp = 5 ml
Tablespoons (tbsp)	1 tbsp = 3 tsp = 15 ml
Fluid Ounces (fl oz)	1 fl oz = 2 tbsp = 30 ml
Cups	1 cup = 8 fl oz = 240 ml
Pints (pt)	1 pt = 2 cups = 16 fl oz = 480 ml
Quarts (qt)	1 qt = 2 pt = 4 cups = 32 fl oz = 960 ml
Gallons (gal)	1 gal = 4 qt = 16 cups = 128 fl oz = 3.8 l
Milliliters (ml)	1 ml = 0.034 fl oz
Liters (l)	1 l = 1000 ml = 4.2 cups
Grams (g)	1 g = 0.035 oz
Ounces (oz)	1 oz = 28.35 g
Pounds (lb)	1 lb = 16 oz = 454 g

What to Eat?

Healthy Fats
Avocados, olive oil, coconut oil, butter, and ghee. Fatty cuts of meat, nuts, seeds, and cheese also provide essential fats for ketosis.

Protein Sources
Opt for high-quality meats (grass-fed beef, vegetarian-fed chicken, turkey), fatty fish (salmon, mackerel), and eggs. Moderate protein intake is key to maintaining ketosis without overloading on protein.

Low-Carb Vegetables
Focus on non-starchy veggies like leafy greens (spinach, kale), cruciferous vegetables (broccoli, cauliflower), zucchini, bell peppers, and asparagus. These provide essential vitamins and fiber without excess carbs.

Nuts and Seeds
Almonds, walnuts, chia seeds, flaxseeds, and pumpkin seeds are keto-friendly options that add fiber and healthy fats.

Dairy and Dairy Alternatives
Full-fat options like cheese, heavy cream, and unsweetened almond or coconut milk are good choices, offering fat and protein with minimal carbs.

Keto-Friendly Sweeteners
Use alternatives like stevia, erythritol, or monk fruit to satisfy sweet cravings without impacting blood sugar.

What to Avoid?

Sugary Foods
Avoid sugar, candy, soda, fruit juices, and desserts with added sugars. High-sugar fruits like bananas, apples, and grapes should also be limited.

Grains and Starches
Bread, rice, pasta, oatmeal, and grains (including wheat, corn, and barley) are high in carbs and should be excluded. Substitute with cauliflower rice, zucchini noodles, or other low-carb options.

High-Carb Vegetables
Limit starchy vegetables like potatoes, sweet potatoes, corn, and peas. Stick to low-carb veggies that won't interfere with ketosis.

Legumes
Beans, lentils, chickpeas, and other legumes are high in carbs and should be minimized on keto. Processed Foods and Sugary Condiments Processed snacks, sauces with added sugars, and packaged foods often contain hidden carbs. Read labels carefully and stick to whole, unprocessed ingredients as much as possible.

Most Fruits
While berries (like strawberries and blackberries) can be enjoyed in moderation, high-carb fruits like bananas, mangoes, and apples should be avoided.

Keto-Friendly Substitutions

One of the best things about the keto lifestyle is that you don't have to give up your favorite foods—you just need to swap out high-carb ingredients for keto-friendly alternatives. Here's how to make easy substitutions that keep your meals flavorful and satisfying without breaking your diet:

Carb Substitutes:
Bread: Replace traditional bread with keto-friendly options made from almond flour or coconut flour. You can also use lettuce wraps or cloud bread as a low-carb alternative.
Rice: Cauliflower rice is a popular substitute that works well in stir-fries, bowls, and side dishes. It's easy to make and has a similar texture to rice.
Pasta: Zucchini noodles (zoodles), spaghetti squash, or shirataki noodles are great low-carb alternatives to traditional pasta.

Potato Substitutes:
Cauliflower Mash: Cauliflower is a versatile low-carb vegetable that can be mashed as a substitute for potatoes. It's creamy and delicious.
Turnips and Radishes: Roasted turnips or radishes can mimic the texture of potatoes in stews and roasts.

Sugar Substitutes:
Erythritol: A keto-friendly sweetener that doesn't spike blood sugar. It's great for baking and sweetening drinks.
Stevia and Monk Fruit: Both are natural, zero-carb sweeteners that can be used in coffee, tea, or desserts without affecting ketosis.

Dairy Substitutes:
Almond Milk: Unsweetened almond milk is a low-carb replacement for regular milk, which is high in lactose and carbs.
Coconut Milk: Full-fat coconut milk or coconut cream is a rich and creamy alternative that's great in keto recipes.

Snack Substitutes:
Chips and Crackers: Swap potato chips for pork rinds or cheese crisps for a crunchy snack.
Popcorn: While regular popcorn is high in carbs, you can try cheese puffs, roasted seaweed, or nuts for a salty snack.
Crackers: Seed crackers made with flax or chia seeds are a keto-friendly alternative to traditional crackers. With these substitutions, you can still enjoy the flavors and textures you love while sticking to your keto goals.

Core Keto Recipes for Every Meal

Welcome to the heart of this cookbook — your go-to collection of delicious, easy-to-make, keto-friendly meals! These recipes have been carefully crafted to help you enjoy a wide variety of flavors while sticking to your keto goals. From energizing breakfasts to satisfying dinners, snacks, and desserts, you'll find everything you need to stay full, happy, and in ketosis.

Breakfast Recipes to Energize Your Mornings

Breakfast is the most important meal of the day, and on keto, it's also one of the most delicious! These breakfast recipes are designed to give you the fuel you need to start your day on the right foot. Whether you prefer something quick and easy or a hearty weekend brunch, there's a recipe here for every morning mood. Each dish is packed with healthy fats and protein to keep you satisfied and full of energy.

Pancakes with Butter and Syrup

Prep. time: 5 min | Cooking time: 10 min | Servings: 4
Ingredients:
• 1 cup (120g) almond flour • 2 large eggs
• 1/4 cup (60ml) unsweetened almond milk
• 1 tsp baking powder • 1 tsp vanilla extract
• 1 tbsp erythritol or another keto-friendly sweetener
• 2 tbsp butter (for cooking) • Optional toppings: Butter, sugar-free syrup, fresh berries
Instructions:
1. Prepare the Batter: • In a mixing bowl, whisk together the almond flour, baking powder, and erythritol
• In another bowl, whisk the eggs, almond milk, and vanilla extract • Combine the wet and dry ingredients, mixing until a smooth batter forms.
2. Cook the Pancakes: • Heat a non-stick skillet or griddle over medium heat and add butter • Pour about 1/4 cup of batter onto the skillet for each pancake • Cook for 2-3 minutes on one side, until bubbles form on the surface, then flip and cook for an additional 1-2 minutes until golden brown.
3. Serve warm with a pat of butter and a drizzle of sugar-free syrup. Add fresh berries if desired.
Nutritional Information (Per Serving):
• Calories: 225 • Protein: 9g • Carbohydrates: 4g
• Fats: 20g • Fiber: 2g • Cholesterol: 110mg
• Sodium: 250mg • Potassium: 120mg • Net Carbs: 2g

These pancakes are perfect with a side of bacon or sausage for a hearty breakfast. Top with your favorite keto-friendly toppings, such as sugar-free syrup, whipped cream, or nuts.

Avocado and Bacon Omelet

Prep. time: 5 min | Cooking time: 10 min | Servings: 2
Ingredients:
• 4 large eggs • 1/4 cup (60ml) heavy cream
• 1/2 avocado, diced • 4 slices bacon, cooked and crumbled • 1/4 cup (28g) shredded cheddar cheese
• 1 tbsp butter • Salt and pepper to taste
• Optional garnish: Fresh chopped parsley, hot sauce
Instructions:
1. In a medium bowl, whisk together the eggs and heavy cream until well combined. Season with salt and pepper.
2. Heat a non-stick skillet over medium heat and add the butter. Once melted, pour the egg mixture into the skillet, tilting to spread evenly • Allow the eggs to cook without stirring until they begin to set around the edges, about 2-3 minutes.
3. Evenly distribute the diced avocado, crumbled bacon, and shredded cheddar cheese over one half of the omelet.
4. Gently fold the other half of the omelet over the fillings. Cook for an additional 1-2 minutes until the cheese is melted and the eggs are fully set.
5. Slide the omelet onto a plate, cut in half, and serve immediately. Garnish with fresh chopped parsley or a dash of hot sauce if desired.
Nutritional Information (Per Serving):
• Calories: 425 • Protein: 22g • Carbohydrates: 4g
• Fats: 36g • Fiber: 2g • Cholesterol: 420mg
• Sodium: 600mg • Potassium: 420mg • Net Carbs: 2g

This omelet pairs well with a side of fresh greens or sliced tomatoes for a complete keto-friendly breakfast. It can also be enjoyed on its own for a satisfying, energy-boosting meal.

Chia Seed Pudding with Almonds

Prep. time: 5 min | Chilling time: 2 hr | Servings: 2

Ingredients:
- 1/4 cup (40g) chia seeds
- 1 cup (240ml) unsweetened almond milk
- 1 tsp vanilla extract
- 1 tbsp erythritol or another keto-friendly sweetener
- 2 tbsp sliced almonds
- Optional toppings: Fresh berries, unsweetened coconut flakes, almond butter

Instructions:
1. Prepare the Pudding: • In a medium bowl, whisk together the chia seeds, almond milk, vanilla extract, and erythritol • Stir until the mixture is well combined and the chia seeds are evenly distributed.
2. Chill: • Cover the bowl and refrigerate for at least 2 hours or overnight, until the pudding has thickened to your desired consistency.
3. Divide the chia pudding between two bowls. Top with sliced almonds and any additional toppings you prefer.

Nutritional Information (Per Serving):
- Calories: 180 • Protein: 6g • Carbohydrates: 8g
- Fats: 12g • Fiber: 7g • Cholesterol: 0mg
- Sodium: 140mg • Potassium: 220mg • Net Carbs: 1g

This chia seed pudding makes a great make-ahead breakfast or snack. Customize it with different toppings to keep it fresh and exciting.

Coconut Flour Waffles with Berries

Prep. time: 5 min | Cooking time: 10 min | Servings: 4

Ingredients:
- 1/2 cup (60g) coconut flour
- 4 large eggs
- 1/4 cup (60ml) unsweetened almond milk
- 1/4 cup (60g) melted butter
- 1 tsp baking powder
- 1 tbsp erythritol or another keto-friendly sweetener
- 1 tsp vanilla extract
- Optional toppings: Fresh berries, sugar-free syrup, whipped cream

Instructions:
1. Prepare the Batter: • In a large bowl, whisk together the coconut flour, baking powder, and erythritol • In another bowl, whisk together the eggs, almond milk, melted butter, and vanilla extract • Slowly mix the wet ingredients into the dry ingredients until a thick batter forms.
2. Cook the Waffles: • Preheat your waffle iron according to the manufacturer's instructions and lightly grease it with butter or oil • Pour the batter into the waffle iron and cook until the waffles are golden brown and cooked through, about 3-5 minutes depending on your waffle iron.
3. Serve hot with your choice of toppings such as fresh berries, sugar-free syrup, or whipped cream.

Nutritional Information (Per Serving):
- Calories: 250 • Protein: 9g • Carbohydrates: 6g
- Fats: 20g • Fiber: 4g • Cholesterol: 185mg
- Sodium: 300mg • Potassium: 150mg • Net Carbs: 2g

These waffles are a satisfying breakfast option and pair well with a variety of keto-friendly toppings. Add a side of scrambled eggs or bacon for a more filling meal.

Spinach and Cheese Frittata

Prep. time: 5 min | Cooking time: 20 min | Servings: 4
Ingredients:
- 8 large eggs • 1/2 cup (120ml) heavy cream
- 1 cup (100g) shredded mozzarella cheese
- 1 cup (30g) fresh spinach, chopped • 1/4 cup (30g) grated Parmesan cheese • 1 tbsp olive oil or butter
- Salt and pepper to taste • Optional: 1/4 cup diced onions, 1/4 cup diced bell peppers

Instructions:
1. Prepare the Egg Mixture: • In a large bowl, whisk together the eggs, heavy cream, salt, and pepper. Stir in the mozzarella and Parmesan cheeses.
2. Cook the Vegetables: • Heat the olive oil or butter in an oven-safe skillet over medium heat. If using, add the onions and bell peppers and cook until softened, about 3-4 minutes • Add the chopped spinach and cook for an additional 1-2 minutes until wilted.
3. Cook the Frittata: • Pour the egg mixture over the vegetables in the skillet. Cook on the stove for 2-3 minutes until the edges start to set • Transfer the skillet to a preheated oven at 375°F (190°C) and bake for 15 minutes, or until the frittata is fully set and slightly golden on top.
4. Slice the frittata into wedges and serve warm. Garnish with fresh herbs if desired.

Nutritional Information (Per Serving):
- Calories: 280 • Protein: 14g • Carbohydrates: 3g
- Fats: 24g • Fiber: 1g • Cholesterol: 310mg
- Sodium: 350mg • Potassium: 300mg • Net Carbs: 2g

This frittata makes an excellent breakfast or brunch option. Pair it with a side salad or keto-friendly toast for a complete meal.

Smoothie Bowl with Nuts and Seeds

Prep. time: 5 min | Cooking time: none | Servings: 2
Ingredients:
- 1/2 avocado
- 1/2 cup (120ml) unsweetened almond milk
- 1/4 cup (60ml) full-fat coconut milk
- 1/4 cup (40g) frozen mixed berries (low-carb berries like raspberries or blackberries)
- 1 tbsp. almond butter
- 1 tbsp. chia seeds
- 1 tbsp. flaxseeds
- 1/4 tsp vanilla extract
- 1/4 tsp cinnamon
- Optional toppings: Sliced almonds, shredded coconut, additional chia seeds, fresh berries

Instructions:
1. Prepare the Smoothie: • In a blender, combine the avocado, almond milk, coconut milk, frozen berries, almond butter, chia seeds, flaxseeds, vanilla extract, and cinnamon • Blend until smooth and creamy.
2. Assemble the Bowl: • Pour the smoothie into a bowl and add your favorite toppings such as sliced almonds, shredded coconut, or additional chia seeds.
3. Serve immediately as a refreshing, nutrient-packed breakfast.

Nutritional Information (Per Serving):
- Calories: 350 • Protein: 7g • Carbohydrates: 10g
- Fats: 30g • Fiber: 8g • Cholesterol: 0mg
- Sodium: 100mg • Potassium: 500mg • Net Carbs: 2g

This smoothie bowl is a versatile breakfast option that can be customized with various keto-friendly toppings to keep it interesting.

Sausage and Egg Muffins

Prep. time: 10 min | Cooking time: 20 min | Servings: 6
Ingredients:
• 6 large eggs • 1/4 cup (60ml) heavy cream
• 1/2 cup (50g) shredded cheddar cheese
• 1/2 lb (225g) ground sausage (pork or turkey)
• 1/4 cup (30g) chopped bell peppers (optional)
• 1/4 cup (30g) chopped spinach (optional)
• Salt and pepper to taste
• 1 tbsp butter (for greasing the muffin tin)
Instructions:
1. Cook the Sausage: • In a skillet, cook the ground sausage over medium heat until browned and fully cooked. Drain any excess grease and set aside.
2. Prepare the Egg Mixture: • In a large bowl, whisk together the eggs, heavy cream, salt, and pepper. Stir in the cooked sausage, shredded cheddar cheese, and any optional vegetables (bell peppers or spinach).
3. Assemble the Muffins: • Preheat your oven to 375°F (190°C). Grease a 12-cup muffin tin with butter • Pour the egg mixture evenly into the muffin cups, filling each about 3/4 full.
4. Bake in the preheated oven for 18-20 minutes, or until the muffins are set and slightly golden on top.
5. Let the muffins cool slightly before removing from the tin. Serve warm.
Nutritional Information (Per Serving):
• Calories: 275 • Protein: 14g • Carbohydrates: 2g
• Fats: 24g • Fiber: 0g • Cholesterol: 230mg
• Sodium: 450mg • Potassium: 180mg • Net Carbs: 2g

These muffins are perfect for meal prepping. Store them in the fridge and reheat for a quick breakfast throughout the week.

French Toast with Cinnamon

Prep. time: 5 min | Cooking time: 10 min | Servings: 4
Ingredients:
• 4 slices keto-friendly bread
• 2 large eggs
• 1/4 cup (60ml) heavy cream
• 1/2 tsp ground cinnamon
• 1/2 tsp vanilla extract
• 1 tbsp butter (for cooking)
• Optional toppings: Sugar-free syrup, butter, fresh berries
Instructions:
1. Prepare the Egg Mixture: • In a shallow bowl, whisk together the eggs, heavy cream, cinnamon, and vanilla extract.
2. Cook the French Toast: • Heat a skillet over medium heat and add butter • Dip each slice of keto bread into the egg mixture, ensuring both sides are coated • Place the coated bread slices in the skillet and cook for 2-3 minutes on each side, or until golden brown.
3. Serve the French toast warm with your choice of toppings such as sugar-free syrup, butter, or fresh berries.
Nutritional Information (Per Serving):
• Calories: 220 • Protein: 9g • Carbohydrates: 5g
• Fats: 18g • Fiber: 3g • Cholesterol: 150mg
• Sodium: 300mg • Potassium: 90mg • Net Carbs: 2g

This keto French toast is a satisfying way to start the day. Pair it with a side of bacon or sausage for a more filling meal.

Bulletproof Coffee

Prep. time: 5 min | Cooking time: none | Servings: 1
Ingredients:
- 1 cup (240ml) hot brewed coffee
- 1 tbsp unsalted butter
- 1 tbsp MCT oil or coconut oil
- Optional: A pinch of cinnamon or cocoa powder

Instructions:
1. Prepare the Coffee: • Brew your coffee as you normally would.
2. Blend: • In a blender, combine the hot coffee, butter, and MCT oil (or coconut oil) • Blend on high for 20-30 seconds until the mixture is frothy and well combined.
3. Pour the bulletproof coffee into a mug and enjoy immediately. Sprinkle with cinnamon or cocoa powder if desired.

Nutritional Information (Per Serving):
- Calories: 210 • Protein: 0g • Carbohydrates: 0g
- Fats: 24g • Fiber: 0g • Cholesterol: 30mg
- Sodium: 10mg • Potassium: 116mg • Net Carbs: 0g

Bulletproof coffee is perfect as a quick, energy-boosting breakfast on the go. It can also be enjoyed alongside other keto-friendly breakfast options.

Zucchini and Cheese Hash Browns

Prep. time: 10 min | Cooking time: 15 min | Servings: 4
Ingredients:
- 2 medium zucchinis, grated
- 1/2 cup (50g) shredded cheddar cheese
- 1/4 cup (30g) grated Parmesan cheese
- 1 large egg
- 1/4 tsp garlic powder
- Salt and pepper to taste
- 2 tbsp coconut oil (for frying)

Instructions:
1. Prepare the Zucchini: • Grate the zucchinis and place them in a clean kitchen towel. Squeeze out as much moisture as possible • In a large bowl, combine the grated zucchini, cheddar cheese, Parmesan cheese, egg, garlic powder, salt, and pepper. Mix well.
2. Form the Hash Browns: • Heat the coconut oil in a large skillet over medium heat • Take a small handful of the zucchini mixture and form it into a patty. Repeat with the remaining mixture • Place the patties in the skillet, cooking for 3-4 minutes on each side, until golden brown and crispy.
3. Serve the hash browns warm, garnished with additional cheese or fresh herbs if desired.

Nutritional Information (Per Serving):
- Calories: 180 • Protein: 7g • Carbohydrates: 4g
- Fats: 16g • Fiber: 1g • Cholesterol: 50mg
- Sodium: 220mg • Potassium: 300mg • Net Carbs: 3g

These hash browns make a great side dish for eggs or breakfast sausage. You can also top them with a poached egg for a more substantial meal.

Breakfast Burrito with Sausage

Prep. time: 10 min | Cooking time: 10 min | Servings: 2
Ingredients:
• 4 large eggs • 1/4 cup (60ml) heavy cream
• 1/2 cup (50g) shredded cheddar cheese
• 2 large sausage links, cooked and crumbled (about 100g)
• 2 tbsp salsa (sugar-free) • 2 large low-carb tortillas
• 1 tbsp butter • Salt and pepper to taste
• Optional toppings: Sliced avocado, sour cream, hot sauce

Instructions:
1. Prepare the Egg Mixture: • In a medium bowl, whisk together the eggs, heavy cream, salt, and pepper.
2. Cook the Eggs: • Heat a non-stick skillet over medium heat and add the butter. Pour in the egg mixture and cook, stirring gently, until the eggs are scrambled and fully cooked. Remove from heat.
3. Assemble the Burritos: • Lay out the low-carb tortillas. Divide the scrambled eggs, crumbled sausage, and shredded cheddar cheese evenly between the two tortillas • Add a tablespoon of salsa to each, then roll up the tortillas into burritos.
4. Serve the burritos warm, topped with sliced avocado, sour cream, and hot sauce if desired.

Nutritional Information (Per Serving):
• Calories: 450 • Protein: 22g • Carbohydrates: 6g
• Fats: 36g • Fiber: 2g • Cholesterol: 330mg
• Sodium: 850mg • Potassium: 400mg • Net Carbs: 4g

These breakfast burritos are a filling, portable meal that's perfect for busy mornings. Pair with a side of fresh greens or enjoy on its own.

Smoked Salmon and Cream Cheese Roll-Ups

Prep. time: 5 min | Cooking time: none | Servings: 2
Ingredients:
• 4 oz (115g) smoked salmon slices
• 4 tbsp cream cheese • 1 tbsp chopped fresh dill
• 1/2 avocado, thinly sliced • 1 tbsp capers (optional)
• 1 tsp lemon juice • Freshly ground black pepper to taste

Instructions:
1. Prepare the Filling: • In a small bowl, mix the cream cheese, chopped dill, and lemon juice until well combined.
2. Assemble the Roll-Ups: • Lay out the smoked salmon slices on a clean surface. Spread the cream cheese mixture evenly over the salmon • Place a few slices of avocado and a few capers (if using) on top of the cream cheese.
3. Roll and Serve: • Gently roll up the salmon slices to form a tight roll. Secure with toothpicks if needed • Sprinkle with freshly ground black pepper and serve immediately.

Nutritional Information (Per Serving):
• Calories: 210 • Protein: 14g • Carbohydrates: 2g
• Fats: 18g • Fiber: 2g • Cholesterol: 45mg
• Sodium: 660mg • Potassium: 330mg • Net Carbs: 0g

These roll-ups are great as a light breakfast or a snack. They pair well with a side of sliced cucumbers or a small salad.

Asparagus and Ham Quiche

Prep. time: 15 min | Cooking time: 35 min | Servings: 6

Ingredients:
- 6 large eggs
- 1/2 cup (120ml) heavy cream
- 1/2 cup (50g) shredded Swiss cheese
- 1/2 cup (50g) diced ham
- 1/2 cup (50g) chopped asparagus
- 1/4 cup (30g) grated Parmesan cheese
- 1 tbsp olive oil or butter
- Salt and pepper to taste
- Optional: 1/4 tsp nutmeg

Instructions:
1. Prepare the Crustless Quiche: • Preheat the oven to 350°F (175°C). Grease a 9-inch pie dish with olive oil or butter • In a large bowl, whisk together the eggs, heavy cream, salt, pepper, and nutmeg (if using). Stir in the Swiss cheese, Parmesan cheese, diced ham, and chopped asparagus.
2. Bake: • Pour the egg mixture into the prepared pie dish • Bake for 30-35 minutes, or until the quiche is fully set and golden brown on top.
3. Let the quiche cool for a few minutes before slicing into wedges. Serve warm.

Nutritional Information (Per Serving):
- Calories: 250 • Protein: 15g • Carbohydrates: 3g
- Fats: 20g • Fiber: 1g • Cholesterol: 250mg
- Sodium: 480mg • Potassium: 220mg • Net Carbs: 2g

This quiche is perfect for a weekend brunch or as a make-ahead breakfast. Serve with a side of fresh greens or a keto-friendly bread.

Almond Flour Muffins with Blueberries

Prep. time: 10 min | Cooking time: 20 min | Servings: 6

Ingredients:
- 1 1/2 cups (180g) almond flour • 2 large eggs
- 1/4 cup (60ml) unsweetened almond milk
- 1/4 cup (60ml) melted butter
- 1/4 cup (50g) erythritol or other keto-friendly sweetener
- 1 tsp baking powder • 1 tsp vanilla extract
- 1/2 cup (75g) fresh or frozen blueberries
- Optional: 1/4 tsp cinnamon

Instructions:
1. Prepare the Batter: • Preheat the oven to 350°F (175°C). Line a muffin tin with paper liners or grease with butter • In a large bowl, whisk together the almond flour, erythritol, baking powder, and cinnamon (if using) • In another bowl, whisk together the eggs, almond milk, melted butter, and vanilla extract • Combine the wet and dry ingredients, then gently fold in the blueberries.
2. Divide the batter evenly among the muffin cups • Bake for 18-20 minutes, or until a toothpick inserted into the center comes out clean.
3. Let the muffins cool in the pan for a few minutes before transferring to a wire rack to cool completely. Serve warm or at room temperature.

Nutritional Information (Per Serving):
- Calories: 200 • Protein: 6g • Carbohydrates: 5g
- Fats: 18g • Fiber: 3g Cholesterol: 55mg
- Sodium: 110mg • Potassium: 60mg • Net Carbs: 2g

These muffins are great for breakfast on the go or as a snack. Pair them with a cup of bulletproof coffee for a complete keto-friendly meal.

Mushroom and Swiss Scramble

Prep. time: 5 min | Cooking time: 10 min | Servings: 2
Ingredients:
• 4 large eggs • 1/4 cup (60ml) heavy cream
• 1/2 cup (50g) sliced mushrooms
• 1/2 cup (50g) shredded Swiss cheese
• 1 tbsp. butter • Salt and pepper to taste
• Optional garnish: Fresh chopped parsley or chives

Instructions:
1. Cook the Mushrooms: • In a non-stick skillet, melt the butter over medium heat. Add the sliced mushrooms and cook for 3-4 minutes until softened and slightly browned.
2. Prepare the Eggs: • In a bowl, whisk together the eggs, heavy cream, salt, and pepper.
3. Cook the Scramble: • Pour the egg mixture into the skillet with the mushrooms. Allow the eggs to set slightly before gently stirring • Continue to cook, stirring occasionally, until the eggs are fully cooked but still soft. Stir in the shredded Swiss cheese until melted and well combined.
4. Serve the scramble immediately, garnished with fresh parsley or chives if desired.

Nutritional Information (Per Serving):
• Calories: 300 • Protein: 15g • Carbohydrates: 4g
• Fats: 26g • Fiber: 1g • Cholesterol: 380mg
• Sodium: 250mg • Potassium: 300mg • Net Carbs: 3g

This mushroom and Swiss scramble pairs well with a side of avocado or keto-friendly toast. It's an easy, satisfying breakfast option that's perfect for busy mornings.

Breakfast Casserole with Bacon

Prep. time: 15 min | Cooking time: 30 min | Servings: 6
Ingredients:
• 8 large eggs • 1/2 cup (120ml) heavy cream
• 1 cup (100g) shredded cheddar cheese • 1/2 cup (50g) diced onions (optional) • 1/2 cup (50g) diced bell peppers (optional) • 1/2 cup (50g) chopped spinach (optional) • 6 slices bacon, cooked and crumbled
• Salt and pepper to taste • 1 tbsp butter (for greasing the baking dish)

Instructions:
1. Preheat the oven to 350°F (175°C). Grease a 9x13-inch baking dish with butter • In a large mixing bowl, whisk together the eggs, heavy cream, salt, and pepper. Stir in the shredded cheddar cheese.
2. Cook the Vegetables (Optional): • In a skillet, sauté the onions and bell peppers in a little butter or oil until softened, about 5 minutes. Stir in the chopped spinach and cook until wilted. Remove from heat.
3. Assemble the Casserole: • Spread the cooked vegetables (if using) and crumbled bacon evenly in the greased baking dish • Pour the egg and cheese mixture over the top, ensuring that the ingredients are evenly distributed.
4. Bake in the preheated oven for 25-30 minutes, or until the eggs are set and the top is slightly golden.
5. Allow the casserole to cool slightly before cutting into squares. Serve warm.

Nutritional Information (Per Serving):
• Calories: 330 • Protein: 17g • Carbohydrates: 3g
• Fats: 28g • Fiber: 1g • Cholesterol: 360mg
• Sodium: 550mg • Potassium: 250mg • Net Carbs: 2g

This breakfast casserole is perfect for meal prepping. Store leftovers in the refrigerator and reheat for a quick and satisfying breakfast throughout the week.

Granola with Coconut and Pecans

Prep. time: 5 min | Cooking time: 15 min | Servings: 4
Ingredients:
• 1/2 cup (50g) unsweetened coconut flakes
• 1/2 cup (50g) chopped pecans • 1/4 cup (25g) sliced almonds • 1/4 cup (25g) pumpkin seeds • 2 tbsp chia seeds • 2 tbsp flaxseeds • 2 tbsp melted coconut oil
• 1 tbsp erythritol or other keto-friendly sweetener
• 1/2 tsp ground cinnamon • 1/4 tsp vanilla extract
Instructions:
1. Prepare the Granola Mixture: • Preheat the oven to 325°F (165°C). Line a baking sheet with parchment paper • In a large bowl, combine the coconut flakes, pecans, sliced almonds, pumpkin seeds, chia seeds, and flaxseeds • Drizzle the melted coconut oil over the mixture and stir in the erythritol, cinnamon, and vanilla extract. Mix until everything is well coated.
2. Bake: • Spread the granola mixture evenly on the prepared baking sheet • Bake for 10-15 minutes, stirring halfway through, until the granola is golden and fragrant.
3. Allow the granola to cool completely before serving. It will become crisp as it cools.
Nutritional Information (Per Serving):
• Calories: 280 • Protein: 5g • Carbohydrates: 7g
• Fats: 26g • Fiber: 6g • Cholesterol: 0mg
• Sodium: 20mg • Potassium: 170mg • Net Carbs: 1g

Enjoy this keto granola with unsweetened almond milk or sprinkle it over a bowl of Greek yogurt for a delicious and crunchy breakfast option.

Egg and Avocado Toast (with Keto Bread)

Prep. time: 5 min | Cooking time: 5 min | Servings: 2
Ingredients:
• 2 slices keto-friendly bread • 2 large eggs
• 1/2 avocado, mashed • 1 tbsp butter
• Salt and pepper to taste • Optional toppings: Red pepper flakes, fresh herbs, lemon juice
Instructions:
1. Toast the Bread: • Toast the keto bread slices in a toaster until golden brown.
2. Cook the Eggs: • In a non-stick skillet, melt the butter over medium heat. Crack the eggs into the skillet and cook to your desired doneness (sunny-side-up, over-easy, etc.).
3. Assemble the Toast: • Spread the mashed avocado evenly over each slice of toast. Season with salt and pepper • Top each avocado toast with a cooked egg.
4. Serve immediately, garnished with optional toppings like red pepper flakes, fresh herbs, or a squeeze of lemon juice.
Nutritional Information (Per Serving):
• Calories: 350 • Protein: 14g • Carbohydrates: 6g
• Fats: 30g • Fiber: 7g • Cholesterol: 225mg
• Sodium: 250mg • Potassium: 450mg • Net Carbs: 0g

This egg and avocado toast is a satisfying breakfast or snack that's perfect for busy mornings. Pair with a side of fresh greens or enjoy it on its own.

Crepes with Cream Cheese Filling

Prep. time: 10 min | Cooking time: 10 min | Servings: 4
Ingredients:
- 1/2 cup (60g) almond flour • 2 large eggs
- 1/4 cup (60ml) unsweetened almond milk
- 2 tbsp melted butter • 1 tsp vanilla extract
- 1 tbsp erythritol or other keto-friendly sweetener
- 1/2 cup (120g) cream cheese • 1 tbsp heavy cream
- Optional toppings: Sugar-free syrup, fresh berries, powdered erythritol

Instructions:
1. Prepare the Crepe Batter: • In a blender, combine the almond flour, eggs, almond milk, melted butter, vanilla extract, and erythritol. Blend until smooth.
2. Cook the Crepes: • Heat a non-stick skillet over medium heat and lightly grease with butter. Pour a small amount of batter into the skillet, swirling to spread evenly • Cook for 1-2 minutes on each side until golden brown. Repeat with the remaining batter.
3. Prepare the Filling: • In a small bowl, whisk together the cream cheese and heavy cream until smooth and creamy.
4. Assemble the Crepes: • Spread the cream cheese filling over each crepe and fold or roll them up • Serve warm with your choice of toppings.

Nutritional Information (Per Serving):
- Calories: 250 • Protein: 8g • Carbohydrates: 5g
- Fats: 22g • Fiber: 2g • Cholesterol: 135mg
- Sodium: 180mg • Potassium: 100mg • Net Carbs: 3g

These keto crepes make for a delightful breakfast or dessert. Customize them with your favorite keto-friendly toppings for a delicious treat.

Cheddar and Herb Biscuits

Prep. time: 10 min | Cooking time: 15 min | Servings: 6
Ingredients:
- 1 1/2 cups (180g) almond flour
- 1/4 cup (50g) shredded cheddar cheese
- 1/4 cup (60ml) heavy cream • 1 large egg
- 1 tsp baking powder • 1/2 tsp garlic powder
- 1/2 tsp dried herbs (such as parsley or thyme)
- 1/4 tsp salt • 2 tbsp melted butter

Instructions:
1. Prepare the Dough: • Preheat the oven to 350°F (175°C). Line a baking sheet with parchment paper • In a large bowl, whisk together the almond flour, baking powder, garlic powder, dried herbs, and salt • Stir in the shredded cheddar cheese • In another bowl, whisk together the heavy cream, egg, and melted butter. Add the wet ingredients to the dry ingredients and mix until a dough forms.
2. Shape the Biscuits: • Drop spoonfuls of dough onto the prepared baking sheet, spacing them about 2 inches apart.
3. Bake for 12-15 minutes, or until the biscuits are golden brown and cooked through.
4. Serve warm, with additional butter if desired.

Nutritional Information (Per Serving):
- Calories: 200 • Protein: 6g • Carbohydrates: 4g
- Fats: 18g • Fiber: 2g • Cholesterol: 55mg
- Sodium: 200mg • Potassium: 60mg • Net Carbs: 2g

These cheddar and herb biscuits are a great accompaniment to any keto breakfast or as a savory snack. Enjoy them with butter or use them as a side for eggs, bacon, or sausage.

Your Lunchtime doesn't have to be boring or complicated on keto! This section features flavorful and filling lunch recipes that are perfect for keeping you energized throughout the day. Whether you're at home or on the go, these meals are easy to prepare and will help you stay on track with your keto goals. From refreshing salads to protein-packed wraps, these lunches are sure to become your favorites.

Lunch Recipes to Keep You Going

Chicken Caesar Salad with Avocado

Prep. time: 10 min | Cooking time: 15 min | Servings: 2
Ingredients:
• 2 boneless, skinless chicken breasts • 2 tbsp olive oil
• 1 tsp garlic powder • Salt and pepper to taste
• 6 cups (150g) chopped romaine lettuce • 1 avocado, sliced • 1/4 cup (30g) grated Parmesan cheese
• 1/4 cup (60ml) Caesar dressing (make sure it's keto-friendly) • Optional: Lemon wedges for garnish
Instructions:
1. Prepare the Chicken: • Preheat a grill or skillet over medium heat • Rub the chicken breasts with olive oil, garlic powder, salt, and pepper • Grill or cook the chicken for 5-7 minutes on each side, or until the internal temperature reaches 165°F (75°C). Let the chicken rest for a few minutes, then slice it.
2. Assemble the Salad: • In a large bowl, combine the chopped romaine lettuce and Caesar dressing. Toss to coat the lettuce evenly • Divide the dressed lettuce between two plates.
3. Add the Toppings: • Top each salad with the sliced chicken breast, avocado slices, and grated Parmesan cheese • Garnish with lemon wedges if desired.
4. Serve immediately as a fresh, satisfying lunch.
Nutritional Information (Per Serving):
• Calories: 450 • Protein: 32g • Carbohydrates: 8g
• Fats: 32g • Fiber: 7g • Cholesterol: 90mg
• Sodium: 550mg • Potassium: 700mg • Net Carbs: 1g

This Chicken Caesar Salad is filling on its own but can be paired with keto-friendly garlic bread or a small bowl of soup for a more substantial meal.

Zucchini Noodles with Pesto and Chicken

Prep. time: 10 min | Cooking time: 15 min | Servings: 2
Ingredients:
• 2 boneless, skinless chicken breasts • 2 tbsp olive oil
• 1 tsp Italian seasoning • Salt and pepper to taste
• 2 medium zucchinis, spiralized • 1/4 cup (60ml) keto-friendly pesto sauce • 1/4 cup (30g) grated Parmesan cheese • 1 tbsp pine nuts (optional) • Optional garnish: Fresh basil leaves, lemon zest
Instructions:
1. Prepare the Chicken: • Preheat a grill or skillet over medium heat • Rub the chicken breasts with olive oil, Italian seasoning, salt, and pepper • Grill or cook the chicken for 5-7 minutes on each side, or until the internal temperature reaches 165°F (75°C). Let the chicken rest, then slice it.
2. Prepare the Zucchini Noodles: • In a large skillet, add a drizzle of olive oil and heat over medium heat
• Add the spiralized zucchini noodles and sauté for 2-3 minutes until just tender • Remove from heat and toss with the pesto sauce.
3. Assemble the Dish: • Divide the zucchini noodles between two plates. Top with sliced grilled chicken
• Sprinkle with grated Parmesan cheese and pine nuts if using.
4. Garnish with fresh basil leaves or lemon zest and serve warm.
Nutritional Information (Per Serving):
• Calories: 400 • Protein: 35g • Carbohydrates: 7g
• Fats: 26g • Fiber: 3g • Cholesterol: 80mg
• Sodium: 400mg • Potassium: 800mg • Net Carbs: 4g

This dish pairs well with a side of roasted vegetables or a small salad. The zucchini noodles make it a light yet satisfying meal perfect for lunch.

Tuna Salad Lettuce Wraps

Prep. time: 10 min | Cooking time: none | Servings: 2
Ingredients:
• 2 (5 oz) cans tuna in olive oil, drained • 1/4 cup (60g) mayonnaise (preferably made with avocado oil)
• 1 tbsp Dijon mustard • 1 tbsp fresh lemon juice
• 1/4 cup (30g) chopped celery • 2 tbsp chopped red onion • 1 small avocado, diced • 8 large romaine or butter lettuce leaves • Salt and pepper to taste • Optional toppings: Sliced cherry tomatoes, chopped fresh dill, capers

Instructions:
1. Prepare the Tuna Salad: • In a medium mixing bowl, combine the drained tuna, mayonnaise, Dijon mustard, lemon juice, celery, and red onion. Mix well.
• Gently fold in the diced avocado and season with salt and pepper to taste.
2. Assemble the Lettuce Wraps: • Lay the lettuce leaves flat on a clean surface • Spoon the tuna salad mixture into the center of each lettuce leaf.
3. Serve the lettuce wraps immediately, garnished with optional toppings like sliced cherry tomatoes, fresh dill, or capers.

Nutritional Information (Per Serving):
• Calories: 350 • Protein: 25g • Carbohydrates: 5g
• Fats: 28g • Fiber: 4g • Cholesterol: 50mg
• Sodium: 450mg • Potassium: 600mg • Net Carbs: 1g

These tuna salad lettuce wraps are a light and refreshing lunch option. Pair them with a side of cucumber slices or a small salad for a complete meal.

Cobb Salad with Blue Cheese Dressing

Prep. time: 15 min | Cooking time: 10 min | Servings: 2
Ingredients:
• 2 boneless, skinless chicken breasts • 4 cups (100g) mixed salad greens • 2 hard-boiled eggs, sliced
• 4 slices bacon, cooked and crumbled • 1 avocado, sliced • 1/2 cup (75g) cherry tomatoes, halved • 1/4 cup (30g) crumbled blue cheese • 1/4 cup (60ml) blue cheese dressing (make sure it's keto-friendly) • Salt and pepper to taste

Instructions:
1. Prepare the Chicken: • Preheat a grill or skillet over medium heat • Season the chicken breasts with salt and pepper • Grill or cook the chicken for 5-7 minutes on each side, or until the internal temperature reaches 165°F (75°C). Let the chicken rest, then slice it.
2. Assemble the Salad: • In a large bowl or on two plates, arrange the mixed salad greens • Top the greens with the sliced chicken, hard-boiled eggs, bacon, avocado, cherry tomatoes, and crumbled blue cheese.
3. Drizzle the blue cheese dressing over the salad.
4. Serve immediately, with additional dressing on the side if desired.

Nutritional Information (Per Serving):
• Calories: 550 • Protein: 35g • Carbohydrates: 10g
• Fats: 42g • Fiber: 6g • Cholesterol: 210mg
• Sodium: 800mg • Potassium: 1000mg • Net Carbs: 4g

This hearty Cobb salad is a meal in itself. For a more indulgent option, add extra blue cheese or bacon.

Bacon-Wrapped Chicken Tenders

Prep. time: 10 min | Cooking time: 25 min | Servings: 4
Ingredients:
• 8 chicken tenders • 8 slices bacon • 1 tsp garlic powder
• 1 tsp smoked paprika • 1/2 tsp black pepper
• 1/2 tsp salt • 1 tbsp olive oil (for brushing)

Instructions:
1. Preheat your oven to 400°F (200°C). Line a baking sheet with parchment paper.
2. Season the Chicken: • In a small bowl, combine the garlic powder, smoked paprika, black pepper, and salt. Sprinkle this seasoning mix evenly over the chicken tenders.
3. Wrap the Chicken: • Wrap each seasoned chicken tender with a slice of bacon, ensuring the bacon overlaps slightly to secure it in place. You can use toothpicks to hold the bacon in place if needed.
4. Bake the Chicken: • Place the bacon-wrapped chicken tenders on the prepared baking sheet. Brush each with a little olive oil to help them crisp up in the oven • Bake for 20-25 minutes, or until the bacon is crispy and the chicken is cooked through. The internal temperature of the chicken should reach 165°F (75°C).
5. Serve the bacon-wrapped chicken tenders hot, with your favorite keto-friendly dipping sauce or alongside a fresh salad.

Nutritional Information (Per Serving):
• Calories: 320 • Protein: 30g • Carbohydrates: 1g
• Fats: 22g • Fiber: 0g • Cholesterol: 85mg
• Sodium: 750mg • Potassium: 400mg • Net Carbs: 1g

These bacon-wrapped chicken tenders are a versatile option for lunch or dinner. Pair them with roasted vegetables, a crisp salad, or even keto-friendly coleslaw for a satisfying meal.

Shrimp and Avocado Salad

Prep. time: 10 min | Cooking time: 5 min | Servings: 2
Ingredients:
• 12 large shrimp, peeled and deveined • 1 tbsp olive oil
• 1 tsp garlic powder • 1/4 tsp paprika • Salt and pepper to taste • 4 cups (100g) mixed salad greens • 1 avocado, sliced • 1/4 cup (60g) cherry tomatoes, halved • 2 tbsp red onion, thinly sliced • 2 tbsp fresh cilantro, chopped (optional) • 2 tbsp lime juice • 2 tbsp olive oil • Optional garnish: Lime wedges

Instructions:
1. Cook the Shrimp: • In a skillet, heat the olive oil over medium heat. Season the shrimp with garlic powder, paprika, salt, and pepper • Add the shrimp to the skillet and cook for 2-3 minutes on each side until they are pink and opaque. Remove from heat and set aside.
2. Prepare the Salad: • In a large bowl, combine the mixed salad greens, avocado slices, cherry tomatoes, red onion, and cilantro (if using).
3. Dress the Salad: • In a small bowl, whisk together the lime juice and olive oil. Drizzle the dressing over the salad and toss gently to combine.
4. Assemble the Dish: • Divide the salad between two plates and top with the cooked shrimp.
5. Serve immediately, garnished with lime wedges if desired.

Nutritional Information (Per Serving):
• Calories: 340 • Protein: 25g • Carbohydrates: 8g
• Fats: 24g • Fiber: 6g • Cholesterol: 190mg
• Sodium: 600mg • Potassium: 700mg • Net Carbs: 2g

This shrimp and avocado salad is a light, refreshing meal perfect for lunch. It pairs well with a keto-friendly soup or a side of grilled vegetables.

Broccoli and Cheddar Soup

Prep. time: 10 min | Cooking time: 20 | Servings: 4

Ingredients:
- 4 cups (240g) fresh broccoli florets • 1 tbsp butter
- 1/2 cup (60g) diced onion • 2 cloves garlic, minced
- 4 cups (960ml) chicken or vegetable broth • 1 cup (240ml) heavy cream • 2 cups (200g) shredded cheddar cheese • Salt and pepper to taste • Optional garnish: Extra shredded cheese, chopped chives, or bacon bits

Instructions:
1. Cook the Broccoli: • In a large pot, melt the butter over medium heat. Add the diced onion and garlic and sauté until softened, about 5 minutes • Add the broccoli florets and cook for another 2 minutes.
2. Simmer the Soup: • Pour in the chicken or vegetable broth and bring to a simmer. Cook for 10-15 minutes, or until the broccoli is tender.
3. Blend the Soup: • Using an immersion blender or a regular blender, puree the soup until smooth (or leave it slightly chunky if you prefer). Return the soup to the pot if using a regular blender.
4. Finish the Soup: • Stir in the heavy cream and shredded cheddar cheese. Cook over low heat until the cheese is melted and the soup is heated through. Season with salt and pepper to taste.
5. Ladle the soup into bowls and garnish with extra cheese, chopped chives, or bacon bits if desired.

Nutritional Information (Per Serving):
- Calories: 380 • Protein: 15g • Carbohydrates: 7g
- Fats: 32g • Fiber: 2g • Cholesterol: 105mg
- Sodium: 700mg • Potassium: 500mg • Net Carbs: 5g

This broccoli and cheddar soup is comforting and filling on its own but can also be paired with a keto-friendly sandwich or salad for a more substantial meal.

Turkey Club Wraps

Prep. time: 10 min | Cooking time: none | Servings: 2

Ingredients:
- 4 large romaine or butter lettuce leaves
- 4 slices turkey breast (deli-style)
- 4 slices bacon, cooked and crumbled
- 1 avocado, sliced
- 4 slices tomato
- 2 tbsp mayonnaise (preferably made with avocado oil)
- Salt and pepper to taste
- Optional: Pickles, red onion slices

Instructions:
1. Prepare the Ingredients: • Lay out the lettuce leaves flat on a clean surface. Spread a thin layer of mayonnaise over each leaf.
2. Assemble the Wraps: • Layer 2 slices of turkey breast, 1 slice of tomato, a few slices of avocado, and crumbled bacon on each lettuce leaf • Season with salt and pepper to taste.
3. Wrap and Serve: • Roll up the lettuce leaves tightly to form wraps. Secure with toothpicks if needed.
• Serve immediately with pickles or red onion slices if desired.

Nutritional Information (Per Serving):
- Calories: 320 • Protein: 20g • Carbohydrates: 5g
- Fats: 25g • Fiber: 4g • Cholesterol: 55mg
- Sodium: 700mg • Potassium: 600mg • Net Carbs: 1g

These keto turkey club wraps are perfect for a quick lunch. Pair them with a side of keto chips or a small salad for a complete meal.

Grilled Steak Salad with Balsamic Vinaigrette

Prep. time: 15 min | Cooking time: 10 min | Servings: 2

Ingredients:
- 2 small ribeye or sirloin steaks (about 6 oz each)
- 2 tbsp olive oil • Salt and pepper to taste
- 4 cups (100g) mixed salad greens • 1/2 cup (75g) cherry tomatoes, halved • 1/2 cucumber, sliced
- 1/4 cup (30g) crumbled blue cheese or feta cheese
- 1/4 cup (60ml) balsamic vinaigrette (make sure it's keto-friendly) • Optional garnish: Fresh basil or parsley

Instructions:
1. Prepare the Steaks: • Preheat a grill or skillet over medium-high heat • Rub the steaks with olive oil, salt, and pepper • Grill or cook the steaks for 4-5 minutes on each side for medium-rare, or until cooked to your desired doneness. Let the steaks rest for a few minutes, then slice thinly.
2. Prepare the Salad: • In a large bowl, combine the mixed salad greens, cherry tomatoes, cucumber, and crumbled cheese.
3. Drizzle the balsamic vinaigrette over the salad and toss to coat the greens evenly.
4. Assemble the Dish: • Divide the salad between two plates. Top with the sliced steak.
5. Serve immediately, garnished with fresh basil or parsley if desired.

Nutritional Information (Per Serving):
- Calories: 500 • Protein: 35g • Carbohydrates: 8g
- Fats: 36g • Fiber: 4g • Cholesterol: 85mg
- Sodium: 600mg • Potassium: 900mg • Net Carbs: 4g

This grilled steak salad is hearty enough to be a standalone meal, but it can also be paired with a keto-friendly soup or bread for a more complete lunch.

Caprese Stuffed Avocados

Prep. time: 10 min | Cooking time: none | Servings: 2

Ingredients:
- 2 ripe avocados, halved and pitted
- 1/2 cup (75g) cherry tomatoes, diced
- 1/4 cup (60g) fresh mozzarella balls (bocconcini), halved • 2 tbsp fresh basil, chopped • 1 tbsp olive oil
- 1 tbsp balsamic vinegar (make sure it's keto-friendly)
- Salt and pepper to taste

Instructions:
1. Prepare the Caprese Salad: • In a small bowl, combine the diced cherry tomatoes, halved mozzarella balls, chopped basil, olive oil, balsamic vinegar, salt, and pepper. Toss gently to combine.
2. Stuff the Avocados: • Scoop a small amount of avocado flesh out of each avocado half to create a larger cavity • Fill each avocado half with the Caprese salad mixture.
3. Serve immediately as a fresh and flavorful lunch option.

Nutritional Information (Per Serving):
- Calories: 350 • Protein: 7g • Carbohydrates: 10g
- Fats: 32g • Fiber: 8g • Cholesterol: 15mg
- Sodium: 150mg • Potassium: 850mg • Net Carbs: 2g

These Caprese stuffed avocados are perfect as a light lunch on their own. For a more substantial meal, pair them with grilled chicken or a side salad.

Chili with Sour Cream

Prep. time: 15 min | Cooking time: 1 hour | Servings: 4

Ingredients:
- 1 lb (450g) ground beef • 1 tbsp olive oil
- 1/2 cup (75g) diced onion • 1/2 cup (75g) diced bell pepper • 2 cloves garlic, minced • 2 tbsp chili powder
- 1 tsp cumin • 1/2 tsp paprika • 1/2 tsp oregano
- 1 (14.5 oz) can diced tomatoes (no added sugar)
- 1 cup (240ml) beef broth • 1/4 cup (60g) tomato paste
- Salt and pepper to taste • 1/4 cup (60g) sour cream
- Optional toppings: Shredded cheddar cheese, sliced jalapeños, chopped cilantro

Instructions:
1. In a large pot, heat the olive oil over medium heat. Add the ground beef and cook until browned, breaking it up with a spoon as it cooks. Drain any excess fat.
2. Add the diced onion, bell pepper, and garlic to the pot with the beef. Cook for 5 minutes until the vegetables are softened.
3. Season the Chili: • Stir in the chili powder, cumin, paprika, oregano, salt, and pepper. Cook for 1-2 minutes until fragrant.
4. Add the diced tomatoes, beef broth, and tomato paste. Stir to combine • Bring the chili to a simmer, then reduce the heat to low. Cover and cook for 45 minutes to 1 hour, stirring occasionally.
5. Ladle the chili into bowls and top each serving with a dollop of sour cream. Add any additional toppings you like, such as shredded cheddar cheese or sliced jalapeños.

Nutritional Information (Per Serving):
- Calories: 350 • Protein: 25g • Carbohydrates: 10g
- Fats: 22g • Fiber: 3g • Cholesterol: 85mg
- Sodium: 650mg • Potassium: 700mg • Net Carbs: 7g

Egg Salad on Keto Bread

Prep. time: 10 min | Cooking time: none | Servings: 2

Ingredients:
- 4 large eggs, hard-boiled and chopped
- 1/4 cup (60g) mayonnaise (preferably made with avocado oil)
- 1 tsp Dijon mustard
- 1 tbsp chopped fresh chives
- Salt and pepper to taste
- 4 slices keto-friendly bread
- Optional garnish: Lettuce leaves, sliced tomatoes

Instructions:
1. Prepare the Egg Salad: • In a medium bowl, combine the chopped hard-boiled eggs, mayonnaise, Dijon mustard, and chopped chives. Mix well • Season with salt and pepper to taste.
2. Assemble the Sandwiches: • Spread the egg salad evenly over two slices of keto bread • Top with lettuce leaves and sliced tomatoes if desired.
3. Serve immediately as a classic and satisfying lunch option.

Nutritional Information (Per Serving):
- Calories: 400 • Protein: 35g • Carbohydrates: 7g
- Fats: 26g • Fiber: 3g • Cholesterol: 80mg
- Sodium: 400mg • Potassium: 800mg • Net Carbs: 4g

This egg salad on keto bread is perfect for a quick and easy lunch. Pair it with a side of fresh cucumber slices or a small salad for a more complete meal.

Keto BLT Salad

Prep. time: 10 min | Cooking time: 10 min | Servings: 2
Ingredients:
• 6 slices bacon • 4 cups (100g) chopped romaine lettuce
• 1 avocado, diced • 1 cup (150g) cherry tomatoes, halved
• 1/4 cup (60ml) creamy ranch dressing (make sure it's keto-friendly) • Salt and pepper to taste
• Optional garnish: Freshly chopped herbs, such as parsley or chives

Instructions:
1. Cook the Bacon: • In a skillet, cook the bacon over medium heat until it's crispy. Transfer the cooked bacon to a paper towel-lined plate to drain any excess grease. Once cooled, crumble the bacon into bite-sized pieces.
2. Assemble the Salad: • In a large salad bowl, combine the chopped romaine lettuce, diced avocado, cherry tomatoes, and crumbled bacon.
3. Dress the Salad: • Drizzle the creamy ranch dressing over the salad. Toss gently to ensure all ingredients are evenly coated. Season with salt and pepper to taste.
4. Divide the salad between two bowls or plates. Garnish with freshly chopped herbs if desired. Serve immediately.

Nutritional Information (Per Serving):
• Calories: 450 • Protein: 12g • Carbohydrates: 8g
• Fats: 40g • Fiber: 6g • Cholesterol: 40mg
• Sodium: 850mg • Potassium: 700mg • Net Carbs: 2g

This Keto BLT Salad is a refreshing and flavorful option that can stand alone as a satisfying meal. For a heartier option, consider adding a boiled egg or a grilled chicken breast on top.

Cauliflower Fried Rice with Pork

Prep. time: 10 min | Cooking time: 15 min | Servings: 4
Ingredients:
• 1 lb (450g) ground pork • 4 cups (400g) cauliflower rice (store-bought or homemade) • 2 tbsp sesame oil, divided • 1/2 cup (75g) diced onion • 1/2 cup (75g) diced bell pepper • 2 cloves garlic, minced • 2 tbsp soy sauce or coconut aminos (ensure it's keto-friendly)
• 1 tbsp rice vinegar • 2 large eggs, lightly beaten
• 1/4 cup (30g) chopped green onions • 1 tbsp sesame seeds (optional) • Salt and pepper to taste

Instructions:
1. Heat 1 tablespoon of sesame oil in a large skillet or wok over medium heat. Add the ground pork and cook until browned and fully cooked, breaking it into small pieces as it cooks. Season with salt and pepper. Once cooked, remove the pork from the skillet and set aside.
2. In the same skillet, add the remaining tablespoon of sesame oil. Sauté the diced onion, bell pepper, and minced garlic for about 3-4 minutes, or until the vegetables are softened and fragrant.
3. Stir the cauliflower rice into the skillet with the vegetables. Cook for 5-7 minutes, stirring occasionally, until the cauliflower is tender and slightly browned.
4. Incorporate the Eggs: • Push the cauliflower mixture to one side of the skillet, creating an empty space. Pour the beaten eggs into the empty space and scramble until fully cooked. Once cooked, stir the scrambled eggs into the cauliflower mixture.
5. Return the cooked pork to the skillet. Stir in the soy sauce or coconut aminos and rice vinegar. Cook for an additional 2-3 minutes, allowing the flavors to meld together. • Stir in the chopped green onions and sesame seeds if using.
6. Serve the cauliflower fried rice hot, garnished with extra green onions or sesame seeds if desired.

Nutritional Information (Per Serving):
• Calories: 320
• Protein: 20g
• Carbohydrates: 7g
• Fats: 24g
• Fiber: 3g
• Potassium: 550mg
• Net Carbs: 4g

Turkey and Cheese Roll-Ups

Prep. time: 5min | Cooking time: none | Servings: 2
Ingredients:
- 8 slices deli turkey breast
- 4 slices cheddar cheese
- 4 leaves romaine lettuce
- 1/2 avocado, thinly sliced
- 2 tbsp mayonnaise (preferably made with avocado oil)
- 1 tbsp Dijon mustard
- Salt and pepper to taste
- Optional: Pickle spears, sliced red onion

Instructions:
1. Prepare the Ingredients: • Lay out the turkey slices on a clean surface. Spread a thin layer of mayonnaise and Dijon mustard over each slice.
2. Assemble the Roll-Ups: • Place a slice of cheddar cheese on top of each turkey slice • Add a lettuce leaf and a few slices of avocado to each, then sprinkle with salt and pepper to taste • Roll up each turkey slice tightly to form a roll-up.
3. Serve the turkey and cheese roll-ups immediately, with pickle spears or sliced red onion on the side if desired.

Nutritional Information (Per Serving):
- Calories: 350 • Protein: 28g • Carbohydrates: 4g
- Fats: 25g • Fiber: 3g • Cholesterol: 75mg
- Sodium: 850mg • Potassium: 450mg • Net Carbs: 1g

These turkey and cheese roll-ups are perfect for a quick and easy lunch. Pair them with a side of keto chips or a small salad for a more filling meal.

Salmon Salad with Lemon Dill Dressing

Prep. time: 10 min | Cooking time: 10 min | Servings: 2
Ingredients:
- 2 salmon fillets (about 4 oz each) • 1 tbsp olive oil
- Salt and pepper to taste • 4 cups (100g) mixed salad greens • 1/2 cucumber, sliced • thinly sliced avocado
- 1/4 red onion, thinly sliced • 2 tbsp fresh dill, chopped
- 2 tbsp lemon juice • 2 tbsp olive oil • 1 tsp Dijon mustard • Optional garnish: Lemon wedges

Instructions:
1. Cook the Salmon: • Preheat a skillet over medium heat and add the olive oil • Season the salmon fillets with salt and pepper, then place them in the skillet • Cook for 4-5 minutes on each side, or until the salmon is cooked through and flakes easily with a fork. Remove from heat and let cool slightly.
2. Prepare the Salad: • In a large bowl, combine the mixed salad greens, cucumber slices, cherry tomatoes, and red onion.
3. Make the Dressing: • In a small bowl, whisk together the lemon juice, olive oil, Dijon mustard, and chopped dill. Season with salt and pepper to taste.
4. Assemble the Dish: • Divide the salad between two plates and top with the cooked salmon fillets.
5. Drizzle the lemon dill dressing over the salad and serve immediately, garnished with lemon wedges if desired.

Nutritional Information (Per Serving):
- Calories: 350 • Protein: 28g • Carbohydrates: 5g
- Fats: 25g • Fiber: 2g • Cholesterol: 70mg
- Sodium: 300mg • Potassium: 600mg • Net Carbs: 3g

This salmon salad with lemon dill dressing is a light, nutritious lunch option that pairs well with a side of keto-friendly bread or a cup of soup.

Chicken Salad with Pecans

Prep. time: 10 min | Cooking time: none | Servings: 4
Ingredients:
• 2 cups (300g) cooked chicken breast, shredded or diced
• 1/2 cup (60g) mayonnaise (preferably made with avocado oil) • 1/4 cup (30g) chopped pecans
• 1/4 cup (30g) chopped celery • 2 tbsp chopped fresh parsley • 1 tbsp Dijon mustard • 1 tbsp lemon juice
• Salt and pepper to taste • Optional: Lettuce leaves or keto-friendly bread for serving

Instructions:
1. Prepare the Chicken Salad: • In a large bowl, combine the shredded or diced chicken, mayonnaise, chopped pecans, celery, parsley, Dijon mustard, and lemon juice • Mix well until all ingredients are evenly coated. Season with salt and pepper to taste.
2. Serve the chicken salad on its own, in lettuce leaves as wraps, or on keto-friendly bread as a sandwich.

Nutritional Information (Per Serving):
• Calories: 350 • Protein: 25g • Carbohydrates: 3g
• Fats: 27g • Fiber: 1g • Cholesterol: 80mg
• Sodium: 350mg • Potassium: 300mg • Net Carbs: 2g

This keto chicken salad with pecans is a versatile lunch option. It can be enjoyed as a light meal on its own or paired with a side of fresh vegetables for a more filling dish.

Beef Taco Salad with Avocado

Prep. time: 10 min | Cooking time: 10 | Servings: 4
Ingredients:
• 1 lb (450g) ground beef • 1 tbsp olive oil
• 2 tsp taco seasoning (make sure it's keto-friendly)
• 4 cups (100g) chopped romaine lettuce
• 1 cup (150g) cherry tomatoes, halved
• 1/2 cup (60g) shredded cheddar cheese
• 1 avocado, diced • 1/4 cup (60ml) sour cream
• 1/4 cup (60ml) salsa (make sure it's keto-friendly)
• Optional garnish: Fresh cilantro, sliced jalapeños

Instructions:
1. Cook the Beef: • In a skillet, heat the olive oil over medium heat. Add the ground beef and cook until browned, breaking it up with a spoon as it cooks • Stir in the taco seasoning and cook for an additional 2-3 minutes until fully combined and heated through.
2. Assemble the Salad: • In a large bowl, combine the chopped romaine lettuce, cherry tomatoes, and shredded cheddar cheese • Top the salad with the cooked ground beef.
3. Add the Toppings: • Top the salad with diced avocado, a dollop of sour cream, and salsa • Garnish with fresh cilantro and sliced jalapeños if desired.
4. Serve immediately, tossing the salad before eating to distribute the flavors.

Nutritional Information (Per Serving):
• Calories: 450 • Protein: 25g • Carbohydrates: 7g
• Fats: 35g • Fiber: 5g • Cholesterol: 90mg
• Sodium: 600mg • Potassium: 750mg • Net Carbs: 2g

This beef taco salad is a filling and flavorful lunch option. You can serve it with keto-friendly tortilla chips or simply enjoy it as a complete meal on its own.

Spinach and Feta Stuffed Chicken

Prep. time: 15 min | Cooking time: 25 min | Servings: 4
Ingredients:
• 4 boneless, skinless chicken breasts • 1 cup (30g) fresh spinach, chopped • 1/2 cup (75g) crumbled feta cheese • 2 cloves garlic, minced • 1 tbsp olive oil • Salt and pepper to taste • 1/2 tsp dried oregano • 1/2 tsp paprika
Instructions:
• Preheat your oven to 375°F (190°C) • Butterfly each chicken breast by slicing it horizontally, but not all the way through, so that it opens like a book.
2. Prepare the Filling: • In a bowl, mix together the chopped spinach, crumbled feta cheese, minced garlic, salt, pepper, and dried oregano.
3. Stuff the Chicken: • Divide the spinach and feta mixture among the chicken breasts, stuffing it inside the butterfly cut. Fold the chicken breasts closed and secure with toothpicks if necessary.
4. Cook the Chicken: • Heat the olive oil in an oven-safe skillet over medium heat. Add the chicken breasts and sear for 2-3 minutes on each side until golden brown • Sprinkle the paprika over the top of the chicken, then transfer the skillet to the preheated oven. Bake for 20-25 minutes, or until the chicken is cooked through and reaches an internal temperature of 165°F (75°C).
5. Let the chicken rest for a few minutes before slicing. Serve warm.
Nutritional Information (Per Serving):
• Calories: 320 • Protein: 40g • Carbohydrates: 2g
• Fats: 16g • Fiber: 1g • Cholesterol: 120mg
• Sodium: 450mg • Potassium: 600mg • Net Carbs: 1g

This spinach and feta stuffed chicken pairs well with roasted vegetables or a side salad. It's a delicious and elegant option for lunch or dinner.

Meatballs with Marinara Sauce

Prep. time: 10 min | Cooking time: 20 min | Servings: 4
Ingredients:
• 1 lb (450g) ground beef • 1/2 lb (225g) ground pork
• 1/2 cup (50g) grated Parmesan cheese • 1/4 cup (25g) almond flour • 1 egg • 2 cloves garlic, minced
• 1 tsp Italian seasoning • Salt and pepper to taste
• 2 cups (480ml) marinara sauce (make sure it's keto-friendly) • 2 tbsp olive oil (for frying) • Optional garnish: Fresh basil, additional Parmesan cheese
Instructions:
1. In a large mixing bowl, combine the ground beef, ground pork, grated Parmesan cheese, almond flour, egg, minced garlic, Italian seasoning, salt, and pepper. Mix well until all ingredients are evenly combined.
2. Form the Meatballs: • Roll the mixture into small meatballs, about 1 inch in diameter.
3. Heat the olive oil in a large skillet over medium heat. Add the meatballs in batches, making sure not to overcrowd the pan • Cook the meatballs for 4-5 minutes on each side until browned and cooked through. Remove the meatballs from the skillet and set aside.
4. Prepare the Marinara Sauce: • In the same skillet, add the marinara sauce and bring it to a simmer. Return the meatballs to the skillet and spoon the sauce over them • Simmer for an additional 5-10 minutes until the meatballs are heated through and coated in sauce.
5. Serve the meatballs warm, garnished with fresh basil and additional Parmesan cheese if desired.
Nutritional Information (Per Serving):
• Calories: 450 • Protein: 25g • Carbohydrates: 6g
• Fats: 35g • Fiber: 2g • Cholesterol: 120mg
• Sodium: 750mg • Potassium: 500mg • Net Carbs: 4g

Dinner is the perfect time to unwind with a comforting and satisfying meal. These dinner recipes are designed to end your day on a high note, with dishes that are both delicious and nutritious. From classic favorites with a keto twist to new flavors that will excite your taste buds, these dinners are full of healthy fats, moderate proteins, and low carbs to keep you in ketosis.

Dinner Recipes to End Your Day Right

Garlic Butter Shrimp with Zoodles

Prep. time: 15 min | Cooking time: 10 min | Servings: 4

Ingredients:
- 1 lb (450g) large shrimp, peeled and deveined
- 3 medium zucchini, spiralized into zoodles • 3 tbsp unsalted butter • 4 cloves garlic, minced • 1/4 cup (60ml) chicken broth • 1 tbsp fresh lemon juice • 1/4 tsp red pepper flakes (optional • Salt and pepper to taste • 2 tbsp fresh parsley, chopped • Lemon wedges for serving

Instructions:
1. Spiralize the zucchini into noodles using a spiralizer. Set the zoodles aside.
2. In a large skillet, melt 2 tablespoons of butter over medium-high heat. Add the shrimp to the skillet, season with salt and pepper, and cook for 2-3 minutes on each side, or until the shrimp turn pink and are fully cooked. Remove the shrimp from the skillet and set aside.
3. Make the Garlic Butter Sauce: • In the same skillet, add the remaining tablespoon of butter. Once melted, add the minced garlic and sauté for about 1 minute until fragrant. Be careful not to burn the garlic • Pour in the chicken broth and lemon juice, stirring to combine. Add the red pepper flakes, if using. Allow the sauce to simmer for 2 minutes.
4. Add the zoodles to the skillet, tossing them in the garlic butter sauce. Cook for 2-3 minutes until the zoodles are tender but still slightly crisp.
5. Return the cooked shrimp to the skillet, tossing them with the zoodles and sauce until everything is well coated and heated through • Garnish with chopped parsley and serve with lemon wedges on the side.

Nutritional Information (Per Serving):
- Calories: 250 • Protein: 25g • Carbohydrates: 5g
- Fats: 14g • Fiber: 2g • Cholesterol: 225mg
- Sodium: 600mg • Potassium: 650mg • Net Carbs: 3g

Beef and Broccoli Stir-Fry

Prep. time: 10 min | Cooking time: 15 min | Servings: 4

Ingredients:
- 1 lb (450g) beef sirloin, thinly sliced • 3 cups broccoli florets • 2 tbsp avocado oil or olive oil • 3 cloves garlic, minced • 1/4 cup soy sauce or coconut aminos • 1 tbsp rice vinegar • 1 tsp sesame oil • 1/4 tsp red pepper flakes (optional) • 1/4 cup beef broth • 1 tbsp sesame seeds (optional) • 2 green onions, sliced (optional)

Instructions:
1. Prepare the Beef and Broccoli: • Slice the beef into thin strips. Wash and cut the broccoli into small florets.
2. Cook the Beef: • Heat the avocado oil in a large skillet over medium-high heat. Add the sliced beef to the skillet, seasoning with salt and pepper. Stir-fry the beef for about 3-4 minutes until browned and cooked through. Remove the beef from the skillet and set aside.
3. Cook the Broccoli: • In the same skillet, add a bit more oil if necessary, then add the broccoli florets. Stir-fry for about 4 minutes until the broccoli is tender-crisp. Add the minced garlic and sauté for another minute.
4. Make the Sauce: • In a small bowl, whisk together the soy sauce (or coconut aminos), rice vinegar, sesame oil, red pepper flakes, and beef broth.
5. Combine and Serve: • Return the cooked beef to the skillet with the broccoli. Pour the sauce over the beef and broccoli, stirring to combine. Cook for another 2-3 minutes until the sauce has thickened slightly • Garnish with sesame seeds and green onions if desired, and serve immediately.

Nutritional Information (Per Serving):
- Calories: 320 • Protein: 30g • Carbohydrates: 8g
- Fats: 18g • Fiber: 3g • Cholesterol: 80mg
- Sodium: 800mg • Potassium: 750mg • Net Carbs: 5g

Baked Salmon with Lemon and Asparagus

Prep. time: 10 min | Cooking time: 20 min | Servings: 4
Ingredients:
• 4 salmon fillets (6 oz each) • 1 lb (450g) asparagus, trimmed • 2 tbsp olive oil • 2 cloves garlic, minced
• 1 lemon, sliced • Salt and pepper to taste
• Fresh dill or parsley for garnish

Instructions:
1. Preheat your oven to 400°F (200°C). Line a baking sheet with parchment paper.
2. Prepare the Asparagus: • Arrange the asparagus on the baking sheet in a single layer. Drizzle with 1 tablespoon of olive oil, and season with salt and pepper. Toss to coat.
3. Prepare the Salmon: • Place the salmon fillets on the baking sheet with the asparagus. Drizzle the salmon with the remaining olive oil, and sprinkle with minced garlic, salt, and pepper. Top each fillet with a lemon slice.
4. Bake the Salmon and Asparagus: • Bake in the preheated oven for 15-20 minutes, or until the salmon is cooked through and flakes easily with a fork, and the asparagus is tender.
5. Garnish the salmon and asparagus with fresh dill or parsley, and serve immediately.

Nutritional Information (Per Serving):
• Calories: 350 • Protein: 34g • Carbohydrates: 6g
• Fats: 20g • Fiber: 3g • Cholesterol: 80mg
• Sodium: 250mg • Potassium: 850mg • Net Carbs: 3g

Pair this dish with a side of cauliflower mash or a simple mixed greens salad. For a complete meal, add a serving of roasted cherry tomatoes or a side of keto garlic bread.

Keto-Friendly Lasagna with Zucchini Noodles

Prep. time: 20 min | Cooking time: 45 min | Servings: 6
Ingredients:
• 3 medium zucchini, sliced lengthwise into thin strips
• 1 lb (450g) ground beef or ground turkey • 2 cups marinara sauce (sugar-free) • 1 cup ricotta cheese
• 2 cups shredded mozzarella cheese • 1/4 cup grated Parmesan cheese • 1 egg • 1 tbsp olive oil • 1 tsp dried oregano • 1 tsp dried basil • Salt and pepper to taste
• Fresh basil for garnish

Instructions:
1 Preheat your oven to 375°F (190°C).
2. Slice the zucchini lengthwise into thin strips using a mandoline or a sharp knife. Lay the zucchini slices on paper towels and sprinkle with salt. Let them sit for 10 minutes to release excess moisture, then pat dry with additional paper towels.
3. In a large skillet, heat olive oil over medium heat. Add the ground beef or turkey, seasoning with salt, pepper, oregano, and basil. Cook until browned, about 8-10 minutes. Drain any excess fat, then stir in the marinara sauce. Simmer for 5 minutes, then remove from heat.
4. In a bowl, mix the ricotta cheese, egg, and half of the shredded mozzarella.
5. In the baking dish, spread a thin layer of the meat sauce on the bottom. Add a layer of zucchini slices, followed by a layer of the cheese mixture. Repeat the layers until all the ingredients are used, ending with a layer of meat sauce. Top with the remaining mozzarella and Parmesan cheese.
6. Cover the baking dish with foil and bake in the preheated oven for 30 minutes. Remove the foil and bake for an additional 15 minutes, or until the cheese is golden and bubbly.
7. Let the lasagna cool for 10 minutes before slicing. Garnish with fresh basil and serve.

Nutritional Information (Per Serving):
• Calories: 350
• Protein: 28g
• Carbohydrates: 8g
• Fats: 22g
• Sodium: 650mg
• Potassium: 850mg
• Fiber: 2g
• Net Carbs: 6g

Grilled Chicken with Avocado Salsa

Prep. time: 10 min | Cooking time: 15 min | Servings: 4
Ingredients:
• 4 boneless, skinless chicken breasts • 2 tbsp olive oil
• 1 tsp garlic powder • 1 tsp onion powder • 1 tsp ground cumin • 1/2 tsp paprika • Salt and pepper to taste
For the Avocado Salsa: • 2 ripe avocados, diced
• 1 small red onion, finely chopped • 1 jalapeño, seeded and diced • 1/4 cup fresh cilantro, chopped • Juice of 1 lime • Salt to taste
Instructions:
1. Preheat your grill to medium-high heat. Brush the chicken breasts with olive oil on both sides. In a small bowl, mix together the garlic powder, onion powder, cumin, paprika, salt, and pepper. Rub the spice mixture evenly over the chicken breasts.
2. Place the chicken on the grill and cook for 6-7 minutes on each side, or until the internal temperature reaches 165°F (74°C) and the chicken is fully cooked. Remove from the grill and let rest for 5 minutes.
3. Prepare the Avocado Salsa: While the chicken is grilling, prepare the avocado salsa. In a medium bowl, combine the diced avocados, red onion, jalapeño, cilantro, lime juice, and salt. Gently toss to mix.
4. Slice the grilled chicken and top with the avocado salsa. Serve immediately.
Nutritional Information (Per Serving):
• Calories: 400 • Protein: 32g • Carbohydrates: 8g
• Fats: 28g • Fiber: 6g • Cholesterol: 95mg
• Sodium: 450mg • Potassium: 900mg • Net Carbs: 2g

This dish pairs well with a side of sautéed spinach or roasted cauliflower. For a refreshing touch, serve with a side of sliced cucumber or a simple mixed greens salad.

Pork Chops with Creamy Mushroom Sauce

Prep. time: 10 min | Cooking time: 20 min | Servings: 4
Ingredients:
• 4 bone-in pork chops (about 1 inch thick) • 2 tbsp butter • 1 tbsp olive oil • 8 oz (225g) mushrooms, sliced
• 3 cloves garlic, minced • 1/2 cup heavy cream
• 1/2 cup chicken broth • 1 tsp Dijon mustard • Salt and pepper to taste • Fresh parsley, chopped for garnish
Instructions:
1. Prepare the Pork Chops: • Season the pork chops on both sides with salt and pepper. In a large skillet, heat the butter and olive oil over medium-high heat.
2. Cook the Pork Chops: • Add the pork chops to the skillet and cook for 4-5 minutes on each side, or until golden brown and the internal temperature reaches 145°F (63°C). Remove the pork chops from the skillet and set aside.
3. Make the Creamy Mushroom Sauce: • In the same skillet, add the sliced mushrooms and cook for about 5 minutes until they are softened and golden. Add the minced garlic and cook for 1 minute until fragrant
• Pour in the chicken broth and bring to a simmer. Stir in the heavy cream and Dijon mustard. Let the sauce simmer for 3-4 minutes until slightly thickened. Season with salt and pepper to taste.
4. Combine and Serve: • Return the pork chops to the skillet, spooning the mushroom sauce over them. Cook for an additional 2-3 minutes to warm through. Garnish with chopped parsley and serve immediately.
Nutritional Information (Per Serving):
• Calories: 450 • Protein: 30g • Carbohydrates: 5g
• Fats: 35g • Fiber: 1g • Cholesterol: 110mg
• Sodium: 400mg • Potassium: 700mg • Net Carbs: 4g

Shepherd's Pie with Cauliflower Mash

Prep. time: 15 min | Cooking time: 30 min | Servings: 6

Ingredients:
For the Filling: • 1 lb. (450g) ground beef or lamb
• 1 small onion, diced • 2 cloves garlic, minced
• 1 cup carrots, diced • 1 cup celery, diced • 1/2 cup beef broth • 2 tbsp. tomato paste • 1 tsp Worcestershire sauce
• 1 tsp dried thyme • Salt and pepper to taste

For the Cauliflower Mash: • 1 large head of cauliflower, cut into florets • 2 tbsp. butter • 1/4 cup heavy cream
• Salt and pepper to taste • 1/4 cup shredded cheddar cheese (optional)

Instructions:
1. Steam the cauliflower florets until they are tender, about 10 minutes. Drain well and transfer to a food processor. Add the butter, heavy cream, salt, and pepper, and blend until smooth and creamy.
2. In a large skillet, cook the ground beef or lamb over medium heat until browned, about 5-7 minutes. Add the onion, garlic, carrots, and celery, and cook for another 5 minutes until the vegetables are softened • Stir in the tomato paste, beef broth, Worcestershire sauce, thyme, salt, and pepper. Simmer for 5 minutes, until the sauce has thickened slightly.
3. Preheat your oven to 375°F (190°C). Spread the meat filling evenly in the bottom of a 9x9-inch baking dish. Top with the cauliflower mash, spreading it evenly over the filling. If desired, sprinkle the top with shredded cheddar cheese.
4. Bake in the preheated oven for 20-25 minutes, or until the top is golden and the filling is bubbly. Let the shepherd's pie cool for a few minutes before serving.

Nutritional Information (Per Serving):
• Calories: 380
• Protein: 22g
• Carbohydrates: 9g
• Fats: 28g
• Fiber: 3g
• Cholesterol: 90mg
• Sodium: 500mg
• Potassium: 850mg
• Net Carbs: 6g

This keto shepherd's pie pairs well with a side of steamed broccoli or roasted Brussels sprouts. A fresh green salad with a light vinaigrette would also balance the richness of the dish.

Lamb Chops with Garlic and Herbs

Prep. time: 10 min | Cooking time: 15 min | Servings: 4

Ingredients:
• 8 lamb chops (about 1-inch thick)
• 3 tbsp. olive oil
• 3 cloves garlic, minced
• 1 tbsp. fresh rosemary, chopped
• 1 tbsp. fresh thyme, chopped
• Salt and pepper to taste
• 1 lemon, cut into wedges for serving

Instructions:
1. Prepare the Lamb Chops: • Preheat your grill or a large skillet over medium-high heat. Rub the lamb chops with olive oil, then season generously with salt, pepper, minced garlic, rosemary, and thyme.
2. Cook the Lamb Chops: • Place the lamb chops on the grill or in the skillet and cook for about 3-4 minutes per side for medium-rare, or until the desired doneness is reached. Remove from heat and let rest for 5 minutes.
3. Serve the lamb chops hot, garnished with lemon wedges for squeezing over the top.

Nutritional Information (Per Serving):
• Calories: 420 • Protein: 28g • Carbohydrates: 1g
• Fats: 34g • Fiber: 0g • Cholesterol: 90mg
• Sodium: 240mg • Potassium: 400mg • Net Carbs: 1g

These lamb chops pair beautifully with a side of roasted vegetables, such as Brussels sprouts or asparagus, or a fresh arugula salad with shaved Parmesan. For a more substantial side, consider serving them with mashed cauliflower or a cauliflower rice pilaf. A glass of a sparkling water with a lemon slice would complement the flavors nicely.

Cauliflower Crust Pizza with Pepperoni

Prep. time: 10 min | Cooking time: 20 min | Servings: 4
Ingredients:
For the Cauliflower Crust: • 1 large head of cauliflower, riced (about 4 cups) • 1/4 cup grated Parmesan cheese • 1/2 cup shredded mozzarella cheese • 1 large egg • 1 tsp garlic powder • 1 tsp dried oregano • Salt and pepper to taste For the Toppings: • 1/2 cup sugar-free marinara sauce • 1 cup shredded mozzarella cheese • 1/4 cup grated Parmesan cheese • 15-20 slices of pepperoni • 1/2 tsp dried oregano • Fresh basil for garnish (optional)
Instructions:
1. Preheat your oven to 425°F (220°C) and line a baking sheet with parchment paper • Steam the riced cauliflower for about 5 minutes, then place it in a clean kitchen towel and squeeze out as much moisture as possible • In a large bowl, combine the cauliflower, Parmesan cheese, mozzarella cheese, egg, garlic powder, oregano, salt, and pepper. Mix until well combined • Transfer the cauliflower mixture to the prepared baking sheet and press it into a 10-12 inch round crust, about 1/4 inch thick • Bake the crust for 12-15 minutes, or until golden brown and firm.
2. Add the Toppings: • Spread the marinara sauce evenly over the baked crust. Sprinkle with mozzarella and Parmesan cheese, then arrange the pepperoni slices on top. Sprinkle with dried oregano.
3. Return the pizza to the oven and bake for an additional 10 minutes, or until the cheese is melted and bubbly.
Nutritional Information (Per Serving):
• Calories: 320 • Protein: 18g • Carbohydrates: 8g
• Fats: 24g • Fiber: 3g • Cholesterol: 80mg
• Sodium: 720mg • Potassium: 550mg • Net Carbs: 5g

Chicken Alfredo with Broccoli

Prep. time: 10 min | Cooking time: 20 min | Servings: 4
Ingredients:
• 4 boneless, skinless chicken breasts • 2 tbsp olive oil
• 3 cups broccoli florets • 1 cup heavy cream
• 1/2 cup grated Parmesan cheese • 2 cloves garlic, minced • 1/2 tsp garlic powder • 1/2 tsp onion powder
• Salt and pepper to taste • Fresh parsley for garnish
Instructions:
1. Cook the Chicken: • Season the chicken breasts with salt, pepper, garlic powder, and onion powder. In a large skillet, heat olive oil over medium-high heat. Add the chicken breasts and cook for 6-7 minutes on each side, or until golden brown and cooked through. Remove from the skillet and set aside.
2. While the chicken is cooking, steam the broccoli florets until tender, about 5 minutes. Set aside.
3. Make the Alfredo Sauce: • In the same skillet used for the chicken, add the minced garlic and sauté for 1 minute until fragrant. Pour in the heavy cream and bring to a simmer. Stir in the grated Parmesan cheese, and continue to simmer for 3-4 minutes, or until the sauce has thickened. Season with salt and pepper to taste.
4. Slice the cooked chicken breasts and return them to the skillet with the Alfredo sauce. Add the steamed broccoli, tossing everything to coat in the sauce. Garnish with fresh parsley and serve immediately.
Nutritional Information (Per Serving):
• Calories: 480 • Protein: 36g • Carbohydrates: 7g
• Fats: 34g • Fiber: 3g • Cholesterol: 140mg
• Sodium: 500mg • Potassium: 750mg • Net Carbs: 4g

This dish is rich and satisfying on its own, but you can also serve it over a bed of zucchini noodles or with a side of cauliflower rice to soak up the creamy Alfredo sauce.

Stuffed Bell Peppers with Ground Beef

Prep. time: 15 min | Cooking time: 35 | Servings: 4
Ingredients:
• 4 large bell peppers, tops cut off and seeds removed
• 1 lb. (450g) ground beef • 1 small onion, diced
• 2 cloves garlic, minced • 1 cup cauliflower rice
• 1 cup marinara sauce (sugar-free) • 1 cup shredded mozzarella cheese • 1/4 cup grated Parmesan cheese
• 1 tsp dried oregano • Salt and pepper to taste
• Fresh parsley for garnish
Instructions:
1. Preheat your oven to 375°F (190°C).
2. Prepare the Filling: • In a large skillet, cook the ground beef over medium heat until browned, about 5-7 minutes. Add the diced onion and garlic, cooking until softened, about 3 minutes. Stir in the cauliflower rice, marinara sauce, oregano, salt, and pepper. Cook for another 5 minutes until the mixture is well combined.
3. Place the bell peppers in a baking dish, standing upright. Spoon the beef and cauliflower mixture into each pepper, filling them generously. Top each pepper with shredded mozzarella and Parmesan cheese.
4. Cover the baking dish with foil and bake in the preheated oven for 25 minutes. Remove the foil and bake for an additional 10 minutes, or until the cheese is melted and bubbly.
5. Let the stuffed peppers cool for a few minutes before serving. Garnish with fresh parsley and serve.
Nutritional Information (Per Serving):
• Calories: 350 • Protein: 28g • Carbohydrates: 10g
• Fats: 22g • Fiber: 4g • Cholesterol: 90mg
• Sodium: 650mg • Potassium: 850mg • Net Carbs: 6g

Meatloaf with Green Beans

Prep. time: 15 min | Cooking time: 1 hour | Servings: 6
Ingredients:
• 1.5 lbs. (680g) ground beef • 1/2 lb. (225g) ground pork • 1 small onion, finely chopped • 2 cloves garlic, minced • 1/4 cup almond flour • 2 eggs • 1/4 cup sugar-free ketchup • 2 tbsp. Worcestershire sauce • 1 tsp dried thyme • 1 tsp dried oregano • Salt and pepper to taste
• 1/2 cup shredded mozzarella cheese (optional)
• 1 lb. (450g) green beans, trimmed • 2 tbsp. butter
Instructions:
1. Preheat your oven to 350°F (175°C). Line a loaf pan with parchment paper or lightly grease it.
2. In a large mixing bowl, combine the ground beef, ground pork, chopped onion, minced garlic, almond flour, eggs, Worcestershire sauce, thyme, oregano, salt, and pepper. Mix until all ingredients are well incorporated.
3. Transfer the meat mixture into the prepared loaf pan, pressing it down evenly. If desired, sprinkle the top with shredded mozzarella cheese. Spread the sugar-free ketchup evenly over the top of the meatloaf.
4. Place the meatloaf in the preheated oven and bake for about 1 hour, or until the internal temperature reaches 160°F (71°C). If the top starts to brown too quickly, cover it with foil. Remove the meatloaf from the oven and let it rest for 10 minutes before slicing.
5. While the meatloaf is baking, bring a pot of salted water to a boil. Add the green beans and cook for 4-5 minutes until tender-crisp. Drain the beans and return them to the pot. Add the butter and toss to coat, seasoning with salt and pepper to taste.

Nutritional Information (Per Serving):
• Calories: 400
• Protein: 28g
• Carbohydrates: 6g
• Fats: 30g
• Sodium: 550mg
• Cholesterol: 110mg
• Fiber: 2g
• Potassium: 650mg
• Net Carbs: 4g

This hearty meatloaf pairs well with mashed cauliflower or a simple side salad for a complete meal. For a refreshing drink, consider serving sparkling water with a splash of lemon.

Keto-Friendly Chicken Parmesan

Prep. time: 15 min | Cooking time: 25 min | Servings: 4

Ingredients:
- 4 boneless, skinless chicken breasts • 1/2 cup almond flour • 1/2 cup grated Parmesan cheese • 1 tsp garlic powder • 1 tsp dried oregano • Salt and pepper to taste • 2 large eggs, beaten • 1/2 cup marinara sauce (sugar-free) • 1 cup shredded mozzarella cheese • 2 tbsp olive oil • Fresh basil for garnish

Instructions:

1. Preheat your oven to 375°F (190°C). Line a baking sheet with parchment paper or lightly grease it.
2. Prepare the Chicken: • In a shallow dish, mix together the almond flour, grated Parmesan, garlic powder, oregano, salt, and pepper. Dip each chicken breast into the beaten eggs, then coat with the almond flour mixture, pressing it onto the chicken to adhere.
3. Cook the Chicken: • In a large skillet, heat the olive oil over medium-high heat. Add the coated chicken breasts and cook for about 3-4 minutes on each side, or until golden brown. Transfer the chicken to the prepared baking sheet.
4. Spoon marinara sauce over each chicken breast, then top with shredded mozzarella cheese. Bake in the preheated oven for 15-20 minutes, or until the cheese is melted and bubbly, and the chicken is cooked through.
5. Garnish with fresh basil and serve immediately.

Nutritional Information (Per Serving):
- Calories: 450 • Protein: 40g • Carbohydrates: 6g
- Fats: 28g • Fiber: 2g • Cholesterol: 120mg
- Sodium: 600mg • Potassium: 700mg • Net Carbs: 4g

Serve this chicken Parmesan with a side of zucchini noodles or cauliflower rice. A fresh green salad with a light vinaigrette would also complement the dish.

Seared Scallops with Garlic Butter

Prep. time: 10 min | Cooking time: 10 min | Servings: 4

Ingredients:
- 1 lb (450g) large sea scallops • 2 tbsp butter
- 2 tbsp olive oil • 3 cloves garlic, minced
- Juice of 1 lemon • Salt and pepper to taste
- Fresh parsley for garnish

Instructions:

1. Prepare the Scallops: • Pat the scallops dry with paper towels and season both sides with salt and pepper.
2. Sear the Scallops: • In a large skillet, heat the olive oil over medium-high heat. Add the scallops, making sure not to overcrowd the pan. Sear the scallops for about 2-3 minutes on each side, until they are golden brown and opaque in the center. Remove the scallops from the skillet and set aside.
3. Make the Garlic Butter Sauce: • In the same skillet, reduce the heat to medium and add the butter. Once melted, add the minced garlic and sauté for about 1 minute until fragrant. Add the lemon juice and stir to combine.
4. Return the scallops to the skillet, spooning the garlic butter sauce over them. Garnish with fresh parsley and serve immediately.

Nutritional Information (Per Serving):
- Calories: 280 • Protein: 22g • Carbohydrates: 3g
- Fats: 20g • Fiber: 0g • Cholesterol: 80mg
- Sodium: 500mg • Potassium: 450mg • Net Carbs: 3g

These seared scallops are perfect when paired with sautéed spinach or roasted asparagus. For a more substantial meal, serve with cauliflower mash or a side of zucchini noodles.

BBQ Ribs with Coleslaw

Prep. time: 15 min | Cooking time: 2 hour | Servings: 4
Ingredients:
• 2 lbs (900g) pork baby back ribs • 1/4 cup sugar-free BBQ sauce • 2 tbsp olive oil • 1 tbsp smoked paprika • 1 tsp garlic powder • 1 tsp onion powder • 1 tsp salt • 1/2 tsp black pepper For the Coleslaw: • 2 cups shredded cabbage • 1/2 cup shredded carrots • 1/4 cup mayonnaise • 1 tbsp apple cider vinegar • 1 tsp Dijon mustard • Salt and pepper to taste
Instructions:
1. Preheat your oven to 300°F (150°C). In a small bowl, mix together the smoked paprika, garlic powder, onion powder, salt, and pepper. Rub the spice mixture evenly over the ribs.
2. Place the ribs on a baking sheet, meat side up, and cover tightly with aluminum foil. Bake in the preheated oven for 2 hours, or until the ribs are tender.
3. Remove the foil and brush the ribs with the sugar-free BBQ sauce. Increase the oven temperature to 425°F (220°C) and bake for an additional 10-15 minutes, until the sauce is caramelized and sticky.
4. While the ribs are baking, prepare the coleslaw. In a large bowl, combine the shredded cabbage and carrots. In a separate bowl, whisk together the mayonnaise, apple cider vinegar, Dijon mustard, salt, and pepper. Pour the dressing over the cabbage mixture and toss to coat.
5. Slice the ribs and serve with a side of coleslaw.
Nutritional Information (Per Serving):
• Calories: 600 • Protein: 40g • Carbohydrates: 10g
• Fats: 45g • Fiber: 3g • Cholesterol: 140mg
• Sodium: 850mg • Potassium: 900mg • Net Carbs: 7g

Zucchini Lasagna with Ricotta

Prep. time: 20 min | Cooking time: 45 min | Servings: 6
Ingredients:
• 3 medium zucchini, sliced lengthwise into thin strips
• 1 lb (450g) ground beef or ground turkey • 2 cups marinara sauce (sugar-free) • 1 cup ricotta cheese
• 2 cups shredded mozzarella cheese • 1/4 cup grated Parmesan cheese • 1 egg • 1 tbsp olive oil • 1 tsp dried oregano • 1 tsp dried basil • Salt and pepper to taste
Instructions:
1. Preheat your oven to 375°F (190°C).
2. Slice the zucchini lengthwise into thin strips using a mandoline or a sharp knife. Lay the zucchini slices on paper towels and sprinkle with salt. Let them sit for 10 minutes to release excess moisture, then pat dry with additional paper towels.
3. In a large skillet, heat the olive oil over medium heat. Add the ground beef or turkey, season with salt, pepper, oregano, and basil. Cook until browned, about 8-10 minutes. Drain any excess fat, then stir in the marinara sauce. Simmer for 5 minutes, then remove from heat.
4. Prepare the Cheese Mixture: • In a bowl, mix the ricotta cheese, egg, and half of the shredded mozzarella.
5. In the baking dish, spread a thin layer of the meat sauce on the bottom. Add a layer of zucchini slices, followed by a layer of the cheese mixture. Repeat the layers until all the ingredients are used, ending with a layer of meat sauce. Top with the remaining mozzarella and Parmesan cheese.
6. Cover the baking dish with foil and bake in the preheated oven for 30 minutes. Remove the foil and bake for an additional 15 minutes, or until the cheese is golden and bubbly.
7. Let the lasagna cool for 10 minutes before slicing. Garnish with fresh basil and serve.

Nutritional Information (Per Serving):
• Calories: 280
• Protein: 22g
• Carbohydrates: 3g
• Fats: 20g
• Fiber: 0g
• Cholesterol: 95mg
• Sodium: 650mg
• Potassium: 450mg
• Net Carbs: 3g

Keto Beef Stroganoff

Prep. time: 10 min | Cooking time: 30 min | Servings: 4

Ingredients:
- 1 lb (450g) beef sirloin, thinly sliced • 1 tbsp olive oil
- 1 small onion, finely chopped • 2 cloves garlic, minced
- 8 oz (225g) mushrooms, sliced • 1 cup beef broth
- 1/2 cup heavy cream • 2 tbsp sour cream
- 1 tbsp Dijon mustard • 1 tsp paprika • Salt and pepper to taste • Fresh parsley for garnish

Instructions:

1. Cook the Beef: • Heat olive oil in a large skillet over medium-high heat. Add the sliced beef, seasoning with salt and pepper, and cook until browned, about 5-7 minutes. Remove the beef from the skillet and set aside.
2. Cook the Vegetables: • In the same skillet, add the chopped onion and cook for 3 minutes until softened. Add the garlic and sliced mushrooms, cooking for another 5 minutes until the mushrooms are browned.
3. Make the Sauce: • Pour in the beef broth, scraping up any browned bits from the bottom of the skillet. Stir in the heavy cream, sour cream, Dijon mustard, and paprika. Bring to a simmer and cook for 5 minutes until the sauce thickens slightly.
4. Return the beef to the skillet, stirring to coat in the sauce. Simmer for another 5 minutes until heated through. Garnish with fresh parsley and serve.

Nutritional Information (Per Serving):
- Calories: 400 • Protein: 30g • Carbohydrates: 7g
- Fats: 28g • Fiber: 2g • Cholesterol: 120mg
- Sodium: 550mg • Potassium: 750mg • Net Carbs: 5g

Serve this beef stroganoff over cauliflower mash or zucchini noodles for a hearty meal. A side of roasted Brussels sprouts or a fresh green salad would also complement the dish.

Grilled Lemon Herb Chicken Thighs

Prep. time: 10 min | Cooking time: 20 min | Servings: 4

Ingredients:
- 8 chicken thighs, bone-in, skin-on
- 1/4 cup olive oil
- Juice of 2 lemons
- 2 cloves garlic, minced
- 1 tbsp fresh rosemary, chopped
- 1 tbsp fresh thyme, chopped
- Salt and pepper to taste

Instructions:

1. Marinate the Chicken: • In a large bowl, whisk together the olive oil, lemon juice, garlic, rosemary, thyme, salt, and pepper. Add the chicken thighs and toss to coat. Cover and refrigerate for at least 30 minutes, or up to 4 hours for more flavor.
2. Grill the Chicken: • Preheat your grill to medium-high heat. Remove the chicken from the marinade and place it on the grill, skin-side down. Grill for 6-7 minutes per side, or until the internal temperature reaches 165°F (74°C) and the chicken is golden and crispy.
3. Let the chicken rest for 5 minutes before serving. Garnish with additional fresh herbs if desired.

Nutritional Information (Per Serving):
- Calories: 450 • Protein: 28g • Carbohydrates: 2g
- Fats: 36g • Fiber: 0g • Cholesterol: 120mg
- Sodium: 400mg • Potassium: 400mg • Net Carbs: 2g

These lemon herb chicken thighs pair perfectly with grilled vegetables, such as zucchini, bell peppers, or asparagus. For a heartier meal, serve with cauliflower rice or a side of creamy mashed cauliflower. A refreshing lemonade or iced herbal tea would be a great beverage choice.

Keto-Friendly Tacos with Lettuce Wraps

Prep. time: 10 min | Cooking time: 15 min | Servings: 4
Ingredients:
• 1 lb (450g) ground beef or turkey • 1 tbsp olive oil
• 1 small onion, finely chopped• 2 cloves garlic, minced
• 1 tbsp chili powder • 1 tsp ground cumin • 1 tsp paprika
• Salt and pepper to taste • 8 large lettuce leaves (e.g., romaine or butter lettuce) • 1 avocado, sliced
• 1/2 cup shredded cheddar cheese • 1/4 cup sour cream
• 1/4 cup salsa (sugar-free) • Fresh cilantro for garnish

Instructions:
1. Cook the Ground Meat: • In a large skillet, heat the olive oil over medium heat. Add the ground beef or turkey, onion, and garlic, cooking until the meat is browned and the onion is softened, about 8-10 minutes. Drain any excess fat.
2. Season the Meat: • Stir in the chili powder, cumin, paprika, salt, and pepper. Cook for an additional 2 minutes until the spices are well incorporated.
3. Assemble the Tacos: • Spoon the seasoned meat into the lettuce leaves, dividing it evenly. Top with sliced avocado, shredded cheese, sour cream, and salsa.
4. Garnish with fresh cilantro and serve immediately.

Nutritional Information (Per Serving):
• Calories: 380 • Protein: 28g • Carbohydrates: 6g
• Fats: 28g • Fiber: 4g • Cholesterol: 90mg
• Sodium: 600mg • Potassium: 750mg • Net Carbs: 2g

These keto tacos are perfect with a side of cauliflower rice or a simple cucumber salad. For added flavor, consider serving with a side of guacamole or a keto-friendly queso dip.

Chicken Pot Pie

Prep. time: 15 min | Cooking time: 45 min | Servings: 6
Ingredients:
For the Filling: • 1 lb (450g) skinless chicken thighs, diced • 2 tbsp butter • 1 small onion, diced • 2 cloves garlic, minced • 1 cup celery, diced • 1 cup carrots, diced • 1 cup chicken broth • 1/2 cup heavy cream • 1 tsp dried thyme • 1 tsp dried rosemary • Salt and pepper to taste
For the Crust: • 1 1/2 cups almond flour
• 1/4 cup coconut flour • 1/2 cup butter, cold and cubed
• 1 large egg • 1/2 tsp salt • 1/2 tsp garlic powder

Instructions:
1. In a large skillet, melt the butter over medium heat. Add the diced chicken thighs and cook until browned on all sides, about 5-7 minutes. Remove the chicken from the skillet and set aside • In the same skillet, add the diced onion, garlic, celery, and carrots. Cook for about 5 minutes until the vegetables are softened • Stir in the chicken broth, heavy cream, thyme, rosemary, salt, and pepper. Bring to a simmer and cook for 5 minutes until the sauce thickens slightly • Return the cooked chicken to the skillet, stirring to combine. Remove the skillet from heat and set aside.
2. Preheat your oven to 375°F (190°C) • In a food processor, combine the almond flour, coconut flour, and salt. Pulse to mix. Add the cold, cubed butter and pulse until the mixture resembles coarse crumbs • Add the egg and pulse until the dough begins to come together. If the dough is too dry, add a tablespoon of cold water, one at a time, until the dough holds together • Turn the dough out onto a sheet of parchment paper. Place another sheet of parchment paper on top and roll out the dough to about 1/4-inch thickness.
3. Transfer the chicken and vegetable filling into a 9-inch pie dish. Carefully place the rolled-out crust over the filling, trimming any excess. Press the edges of the crust down around the dish to seal. Cut a few small slits in the top of the crust to allow steam to escape.
4. Place the pot pie in the preheated oven and bake for 25-30 minutes, or until the crust is golden brown and the filling is bubbly. Allow the pot pie to cool for 5-10 minutes before slicing.

Nutritional Information (Per Serving):
• Calories: 280
• Protein: 22g
• Carbohydrates: 3g
• Fats: 20g
• Fiber: 0g
• Cholesterol: 110mg
• Sodium: 600mg
• Potassium: 450mg
• Net Carbs: 3g

Keto snacking can be both convenient and tasty! This section is all about keeping your energy levels up with easy, grab-and-go snacks and satisfying appetizers. Whether you're hosting a gathering or just need a quick bite between meals, these recipes will curb your cravings and keep you feeling great throughout the day. All while staying keto-friendly!

Snacks and Appetizers: Keep Your Energy Up

Deviled Eggs with Bacon

Prep. time: 15 min | Cooking time: 10 min | Servings: 6
Ingredients:
- 6 large eggs • 2 tbsp mayonnaise
- 1 tsp Dijon mustard • 1 tsp apple cider vinegar
- 2 slices bacon, cooked and crumbled
- Salt and pepper to taste • Paprika for garnish
- Chopped chives for garnish (optional)

Instructions:
1. Place the eggs in a saucepan and cover with cold water. Bring to a boil over medium heat, then remove from heat and cover. Let the eggs sit for 10 minutes.
2. Prepare the Filling: • Drain the eggs and transfer them to an ice bath to cool. Once cool, peel the eggs and slice them in half lengthwise. Remove the yolks and place them in a bowl • Mash the yolks with a fork, then mix in the mayonnaise, Dijon mustard, apple cider vinegar, salt, and pepper until smooth. Stir in half of the crumbled bacon.
3. Assemble the Deviled Eggs: • Spoon or pipe the yolk mixture back into the egg whites. Sprinkle the tops with the remaining bacon, paprika, and chopped chives if desired.
4. Arrange the deviled eggs on a platter and serve immediately or refrigerate until ready to serve.

Nutritional Information (Per Serving):
- Calories: 100 • Protein: 6g • Carbohydrates: 1g
- Fats: 8g • Fiber: 0g • Cholesterol: 190mg
- Sodium: 150mg • Potassium: 60mg • Net Carbs: 1g

These deviled eggs are perfect for a snack or appetizer. Serve them with a side of pickles or olives for a keto-friendly snack tray. Pair with iced tea or sparkling water.

Parmesan Crisps with Herbs

Prep. time: 5 min | Cooking time: 8-10 min | Servings: 4
Ingredients:
- 1 cup grated Parmesan cheese
- 1 tsp dried Italian herbs (such as oregano, basil, and thyme) • 1/4 tsp garlic powder • 1/4 tsp black pepper

Instructions:
1. Preheat your oven to 400°F (200°C). Line a baking sheet with parchment paper.
2. Prepare the Crisps: • In a small bowl, mix together the Parmesan cheese, dried herbs, garlic powder, and black pepper.
3. Form the Crisps: • Spoon heaping tablespoons of the cheese mixture onto the prepared baking sheet, flattening each spoonful slightly to form a round. Leave space between each round as they will spread slightly during baking.
4. Bake in the preheated oven for 8-10 minutes, or until the crisps are golden and bubbly. Remove from the oven and allow to cool on the baking sheet for a few minutes before transferring to a wire rack to cool completely.
5. Serve the crisps as a snack on their own, or pair with dips like guacamole or marinara sauce.

Nutritional Information (Per Serving):
- Calories: 110 • Protein: 9g • Carbohydrates: 1g
- Fats: 8g • Fiber: 0g • Cholesterol: 20mg
- Sodium: 350mg • Potassium: 30mg • Net Carbs: 1g

These Parmesan crisps are a great snack on their own or served alongside a keto-friendly dip. They also make a wonderful topping for salads or soups. Pair with a glass of sparkling water or a light herbal tea.

Avocado and Tuna Salad Cups

Prep. time: 10 min | Servings: 4

Ingredients:
- 2 ripe avocados
- 1 can (5 oz) tuna packed in water, drained
- 2 tbsp mayonnaise
- 1 tbsp fresh lemon juice
- 1 small celery stalk, finely chopped
- 1 small red onion, finely chopped
- Salt and pepper to taste
- Fresh parsley for garnish

Instructions:

1. Prepare the Avocado Cups: • Cut the avocados in half lengthwise and remove the pits. Scoop out a small amount of the flesh to create a larger cavity for the filling, and set aside.
2. Make the Tuna Salad: • In a medium bowl, combine the drained tuna, mayonnaise, lemon juice, chopped celery, and red onion. Season with salt and pepper to taste. Mix until well combined.
3. Assemble the Salad Cups: • Spoon the tuna salad mixture into the avocado halves, filling them generously.
4. Garnish with fresh parsley and serve immediately.

Nutritional Information (Per Serving):
- Calories: 250 • Protein: 12g • Carbohydrates: 8g
- Fats: 20g • Fiber: 7g • Cholesterol: 20mg
- Sodium: 250mg • Potassium: 700mg • Net Carbs: 1g

These avocado and tuna salad cups make for a refreshing snack or light lunch. Serve with a side of cucumber slices or a simple green salad. A glass of iced tea or a lemon-infused water would complement the dish.

Cheese-Stuffed Mushrooms

Prep. time: 10 min | Cooking time: 20 min | Servings: 4

Ingredients:
- 16 large button mushrooms
- 1/2 cup cream cheese, softened
- 1/2 cup shredded mozzarella cheese
- 1/4 cup grated Parmesan cheese
- 2 cloves garlic, minced
- 1 tbsp fresh parsley, chopped
- Salt and pepper to taste
- Olive oil for drizzling

Instructions:

1. Preheat your oven to 375°F (190°C). Line a baking sheet with parchment paper.
2. Prepare the Mushrooms: • Clean the mushrooms and remove the stems. Place the mushroom caps on the prepared baking sheet.
3. Make the Filling: • In a medium bowl, combine the cream cheese, mozzarella, Parmesan, garlic, parsley, salt, and pepper. Mix until smooth and creamy.
4. Spoon the cheese mixture into each mushroom cap, filling them generously. Drizzle with a little olive oil.
5. Bake in the preheated oven for 15-20 minutes, or until the mushrooms are tender and the cheese is golden and bubbly.
6. Serve the stuffed mushrooms hot, garnished with additional parsley if desired.

Nutritional Information (Per Serving):
- Calories: 180 • Protein: 7g • Carbohydrates: 4g
- Fats: 15g • Fiber: 1g • Cholesterol: 35mg
- Sodium: 300mg • Potassium: 350mg • Net Carbs: 3g

These cheese-stuffed mushrooms are a perfect appetizer or snack. Serve them alongside a fresh green salad or as part of a keto-friendly antipasto platter.

Cucumber Slices with Cream Cheese and Lox

Prep. time: 10 min | Servings: 4

Ingredients:
- 1 large cucumber, sliced into rounds
- 4 oz cream cheese, softened
- 2 oz lox (smoked salmon), sliced into small pieces
- 1 tbsp fresh dill, chopped
- 1 tsp lemon zest
- Salt and pepper to taste

Instructions:
1. Prepare the Cucumber Slices: • Arrange the cucumber slices on a serving platter.
2. Assemble the Toppings: • Spread a small amount of cream cheese on each cucumber slice. Top with a piece of lox, then sprinkle with fresh dill and lemon zest. Season with salt and pepper to taste.
3. Serve immediately as a light snack or appetizer.

Nutritional Information (Per Serving):
- Calories: 120 • Protein: 5g • Carbohydrates: 4g
- Fats: 10g • Fiber: 1g • Cholesterol: 30mg
- Sodium: 200mg • Potassium: 250mg • Net Carbs: 3g

These cucumber slices with cream cheese and lox are light and refreshing. Pair them with a side of olives or a small salad for a more substantial snack.

Nachos with Cheese Crisps

Prep. time: 10 min | Cooking time: 15 min | Servings: 4

Ingredients:
- 2 cups shredded cheddar cheese • 1/2 lb (225g) ground beef • 1 tbsp taco seasoning (sugar-free)
- 1/2 cup salsa (sugar-free) • 1/4 cup sour cream
- 1/4 cup guacamole • 1/4 cup sliced black olives
- 1/4 cup sliced jalapeños • 1/4 cup diced tomatoes
- 2 tbsp chopped fresh cilantro

Instructions:
1. Preheat your oven to 400°F (200°C). Line a baking sheet with parchment paper.
2. Make the Cheese Crisps: • Place heaping tablespoons of shredded cheddar cheese on the prepared baking sheet, spacing them about 2 inches apart. Flatten each pile slightly to form a round. Bake in the preheated oven for 5-7 minutes, or until the cheese is bubbly and golden brown. Remove from the oven and allow the crisps to cool on the baking sheet.
3. In a skillet over medium heat, cook the ground beef until browned, about 5-7 minutes. Drain any excess fat. Stir in the taco seasoning and cook for another 2 minutes. Set aside.
4. Top each crisp with a spoonful of the seasoned ground beef. Add the salsa, sour cream, guacamole, olives, jalapeños, and diced tomatoes.
5. Garnish with chopped cilantro and serve immediately.

Nutritional Information (Per Serving):
- Calories: 350 • Protein: 20g • Carbohydrates: 5g
- Fats: 28g • Fiber: 2g • Cholesterol: 70mg
- Sodium: 600mg • Potassium: 400mg • Net Carbs: 3g

These keto nachos are a great snack or appetizer. Serve them with extra salsa, guacamole, and sour cream on the side for dipping.

Baked Avocado Fries

Prep. time: 10 min | Cook time: 15 min | Serving: 4

Ingredients:
- 2 ripe avocados, sliced into wedges
- 1 egg, beaten
- 1/2 cup almond flour
- 1/4 cup grated Parmesan cheese
- 1/2 tsp paprika
- Salt and pepper to taste

Instructions:
1. Preheat the oven to 425°F (220°C). Line a baking sheet with parchment paper.
2. Dip each avocado wedge into the beaten egg, then coat with a mixture of almond flour, Parmesan, paprika, salt, and pepper.
3. Place the coated wedges on the baking sheet and bake for 12-15 minutes, until golden and crispy.
4. Serve with a low-carb dipping sauce, if desired.

Nutritional Information (Per Serving):
- Calories: 160 • Protein: 4g • Carbohydrates: 4g
- Fats: 13g • Fiber: 3g • Net Carbs: 1g

Make sure the avocados are ripe but firm to hold their shape well during baking. Overly soft avocados may not coat or bake evenly. For added crispiness, turn the avocado fries halfway through baking. Serve these with a side of keto-friendly dipping sauces, such as spicy mayo, garlic aioli, or ranch dressing, for extra flavor.

Bacon-Wrapped Jalapeño Poppers

Prep. time: 15 min | Cooking time: 20 min | Yield: 12 poppers

Ingredients:
- 6 large jalapeños, halved and seeds removed
- 4 oz cream cheese, softened
- 1/2 cup shredded cheddar cheese
- 6 slices bacon, cut in half
- 1/2 tsp garlic powder
- 1/2 tsp onion powder
- Salt and pepper to taste

Instructions:
1. Preheat your oven to 400°F (200°C). Line a baking sheet with parchment paper.
2. Prepare the Filling: • In a small bowl, mix together the cream cheese, shredded cheddar, garlic powder, onion powder, salt, and pepper until smooth.
3. Stuff the Jalapeños: • Spoon the cream cheese mixture into each jalapeño half. Wrap each stuffed jalapeño with a half-slice of bacon, securing with a toothpick if necessary.
4. Arrange the jalapeño poppers on the prepared baking sheet. Bake in the preheated oven for 18-20 minutes, or until the bacon is crispy and the cheese is bubbly.
5. Remove the toothpicks and serve the poppers hot.

Nutritional Information (Per Serving):
- Calories: 110 • Protein: 4g • Carbohydrates: 1g
- Fats: 10g • Fiber: 0g • Cholesterol: 20mg
- Sodium: 250mg • Potassium: 100mg • Net Carbs: 1g

These bacon-wrapped jalapeño poppers are perfect as an appetizer or snack. Serve with a side of ranch dressing or sour cream for dipping.

Spinach Artichoke Dip with Veggies

Prep. time: 10 min | Cooking time: 20 min | Servings: 8
Ingredients:
- 1 cup spinach, chopped
- 1 cup canned artichoke hearts, drained and chopped
- 1/2 cup cream cheese, softened
- 1/2 cup sour cream
- 1/4 cup mayonnaise
- 1 cup shredded mozzarella cheese
- 1/4 cup grated Parmesan cheese
- 2 cloves garlic, minced
- Salt and pepper to taste
- Assorted raw veggies for dipping (e.g., celery, bell peppers, cucumbers)

Instructions:
1. Preheat your oven to 350°F (175°C). Grease a small baking dish.
2. Prepare the Dip: • In a medium bowl, combine the chopped spinach, artichoke hearts, cream cheese, sour cream, mayonnaise, mozzarella, Parmesan, garlic, salt, and pepper. Mix until well combined.
3. Transfer the dip mixture to the prepared baking dish and spread it out evenly. Bake in the preheated oven for 20 minutes, or until the top is golden and bubbly.
4. Serve the dip hot with assorted raw veggies for dipping.

Nutritional Information (Per Serving):
- Calories: 150 • Protein: 4g • Carbohydrates: 3g
- Fats: 13g • Fiber: 1g • Cholesterol: 30mg
- Sodium: 300mg • Potassium: 150mg • Net Carbs: 2g

This creamy spinach artichoke dip is delicious with fresh veggies, but it can also be served with keto-friendly crackers or cheese crisps. Pair with a glass of iced tea or sparkling water for a refreshing accompaniment.

Coconut Macaroons

Prep. time: 10 min | Cooking time: 20 min | Yield: 12 macaroons
Ingredients:
- 2 large egg whites
- 1/4 cup erythritol or your preferred keto sweetener
- 1/2 tsp vanilla extract
- 1 1/2 cups unsweetened shredded coconut
- Pinch of salt

Instructions:
1. Preheat your oven to 325°F (160°C). Line a baking sheet with parchment paper.
2. Prepare the Mixture: • In a medium bowl, whisk the egg whites until frothy. Add the erythritol, vanilla extract, and salt, whisking until combined. Gently fold in the shredded coconut until the mixture is evenly moistened.
3. Form the Macaroons: • Scoop heaping tablespoons of the mixture and form into small mounds on the prepared baking sheet.
4. Bake in the preheated oven for 18-20 minutes, or until the macaroons are golden brown on the edges.
5. Allow the macaroons to cool on the baking sheet for a few minutes before transferring to a wire rack to cool completely.

Nutritional Information (Per Serving):
- Calories: 90 • Protein: 1g • Carbohydrates: 3g
- Fats: 8g • Fiber: 2g • Cholesterol: 0mg
- Sodium: 35mg • Potassium: 60mg • Net Carbs: 1g

These coconut macaroons are a delightful keto-friendly dessert or snack. Enjoy them with a cup of coffee or tea for a sweet treat.

Zucchini Chips with Ranch Dip

Prep. time: 10 min | Cooking time: 2 hours | Servings: 4
Ingredients:
- 2 medium zucchinis, thinly sliced • 1 tbsp olive oil
- 1/2 tsp garlic powder • 1/2 tsp onion powder
- Salt and pepper to taste

For the Ranch Dip: • 1/2 cup sour cream • 1/4 cup mayonnaise • 1 tbsp fresh dill, chopped • 1 tbsp fresh parsley, chopped • 1 tsp garlic powder • 1 tsp onion powder • 1 tbsp lemon juice • Salt and pepper to taste

Instructions:
1. Preheat your oven to 225°F (110°C). Line two baking sheets with parchment paper.
2. In a large bowl, toss the zucchini slices with olive oil, garlic powder, onion powder, salt, and pepper until evenly coated. Arrange the slices in a single layer on the prepared baking sheets.
3. Bake in the preheated oven for 1.5 to 2 hours, flipping halfway through, until the zucchini slices are crispy and golden. Remove from the oven and let them cool completely.
4. Prepare the Ranch Dip: • In a small bowl, whisk together the sour cream, mayonnaise, dill, parsley, garlic powder, onion powder, lemon juice, salt, and pepper. Adjust seasoning to taste. Refrigerate until ready to serve.

Nutritional Information (Per Serving):
- Calories: 120 • Protein: 2g • Carbohydrates: 5g
- Fats: 10g • Fiber: 2g • Cholesterol: 10mg
- Sodium: 250mg • Potassium: 300mg • Net Carbs: 3g

These zucchini chips are a perfect low-carb snack or appetizer. Enjoy them on their own or pair with the ranch dip for added flavor.

Prosciutto-Wrapped Asparagus

Prep. time: 10 min | Cooking time: 15 min | Servings: 4
Ingredients:
- 12 asparagus spears, trimmed
- 6 slices prosciutto, halved lengthwise
- 1 tbsp olive oil
- 1/4 tsp black pepper
- 1 tbsp grated Parmesan cheese (optional)

Instructions:
1. Preheat your oven to 400°F (200°C). Line a baking sheet with parchment paper.
2. Wrap each asparagus spear with a half slice of prosciutto, starting from the base and working your way to the tip. Arrange the wrapped asparagus spears on the prepared baking sheet.
3. Drizzle the wrapped asparagus with olive oil and sprinkle with black pepper. If desired, sprinkle grated Parmesan cheese over the top.
4. Bake in the preheated oven for 12-15 minutes, or until the prosciutto is crispy and the asparagus is tender.
5. Serve immediately as an elegant appetizer or side dish.

Nutritional Information (Per Serving):
- Calories: 110 • Protein: 6g • Carbohydrates: 2g
- Fats: 8g • Fiber: 1g • Cholesterol: 20mg
- Sodium: 300mg • Potassium: 200mg • Net Carbs: 1g

These prosciutto-wrapped asparagus spears are delicious on their own or served with a side of keto-friendly aioli. They make an elegant appetizer or can be paired with a salad for a light meal.

Keto Garlic Knots

Prep. time: 10 min | Cooking time: 15 | Servings: 8
Ingredients:
• 1 1/2 cups almond flour • 2 cups shredded mozzarella cheese • 2 tbsp cream cheese • 1 large egg • 1/2 tsp garlic powder • 1/2 tsp baking powder • 1/4 tsp salt
For the Garlic Butter: • 2 tbsp butter, melted
• 2 cloves garlic, minced • 1 tbsp fresh parsley, chopped
• Pinch of salt
Instructions:
1. Preheat your oven to 375°F (190°C). Line a baking sheet with parchment paper.
2. In a microwave-safe bowl, combine the shredded mozzarella and cream cheese. Microwave on high for 1 minute, then stir until smooth. If needed, microwave for an additional 20-30 seconds until fully melted and combined • In a separate bowl, mix together the almond flour, garlic powder, baking powder, and salt. Add the dry ingredients and the egg to the melted cheese mixture, stirring until a dough forms.
3. Divide the dough into 8 equal portions. Roll each portion into a long rope, then tie into a knot. Place the knots on the prepared baking sheet.
4. Bake in the preheated oven for 12-15 minutes, or until the knots are golden brown.
5. While the knots are baking, mix together the melted butter, minced garlic, chopped parsley, and salt.
6. Brush the hot garlic knots with the garlic butter mixture. Serve warm.
Nutritional Information (Per Serving):
• Calories: 150 • Protein: 8g • Carbohydrates: 3g
• Fats: 12g • Fiber: 2g • Cholesterol: 40mg
• Sodium: 250mg • Potassium: 50mg • Net Carbs: 1g

Buffalo Chicken Dip

Prep. time: 10 min | Cooking time: 20 min | Servings: 6
Ingredients:
• 2 cups shredded cooked chicken
• 8 oz cream cheese, softened
• 1/2 cup sour cream
• 1/2 cup buffalo sauce
• 1/2 cup shredded cheddar cheese
• 1/4 cup blue cheese crumbles
• 2 tbsp green onions, chopped
Instructions:
1. Preheat your oven to 375°F (190°C). Grease a small baking dish.
2. Prepare the Dip: • In a medium bowl, mix together the shredded chicken, cream cheese, sour cream, buffalo sauce, and cheddar cheese until well combined. Transfer the mixture to the prepared baking dish.
3. Bake in the preheated oven for 15-20 minutes, or until the dip is bubbly and heated through.
4. Garnish with blue cheese crumbles and chopped green onions. Serve hot with celery sticks, cucumber slices, or keto-friendly crackers.
Nutritional Information (Per Serving):
• Calories: 250 • Protein: 15g • Carbohydrates: 3g
• Fats: 20g • Fiber: 1g • Cholesterol: 70mg
• Sodium: 600mg • Potassium: 200mg • Net Carbs: 2g

This keto buffalo chicken dip is a perfect appetizer for game day or gatherings. Serve it with crunchy veggies or cheese crisps for dipping. Pair with a cold keto-friendly beer or sparkling water with lime.

Chocolate Almond Fat Bombs

Prep. time: 10 min | Freezing time: 30 min | Yield: 12 fat bombs

Ingredients:
- 1/2 cup almond butter (unsweetened)
- 1/4 cup coconut oil, melted
- 2 tbsp unsweetened cocoa powder
- 1-2 tbsp erythritol or your preferred keto sweetener
- 1/2 tsp vanilla extract
- Pinch of salt

Instructions:
1. Prepare the Mixture: • In a medium bowl, combine the almond butter, melted coconut oil, cocoa powder, erythritol, vanilla extract, and salt. Mix until smooth and well combined.
2. Form the Fat Bombs: • Pour the mixture into silicone molds or mini muffin liners. Freeze for at least 30 minutes, or until solid.
3. Once frozen, remove the fat bombs from the molds and store them in an airtight container in the freezer. Serve chilled.

Nutritional Information (Per Serving):
- Calories: 100 • Protein: 2g • Carbohydrates: 2g
- Fats: 10g • Fiber: 1g • Cholesterol: 0mg
- Sodium: 20mg • Potassium: 100mg • Net Carbs: 1g

These chocolate almond fat bombs are perfect for a quick snack or dessert. Enjoy them with a cup of hot coffee or tea for a satisfying keto treat.

Cheese and Olive Skewers

Prep. time: 10 min | Servings: 4

Ingredients:
- 16 small mozzarella balls (bocconcini) or cubes of your favorite cheese
- 16 pitted olives (green or black)
- 16 grape or cherry tomatoes
- Fresh basil leaves
- 2 tbsp extra virgin olive oil
- 1 tbsp balsamic vinegar
- Salt and pepper to taste
- 16 small wooden skewers

Instructions:
1. Assemble the Skewers: • On each skewer, alternate between a mozzarella ball, olive, tomato, and basil leaf. Repeat until all skewers are assembled.
2. Drizzle and Season: • Arrange the skewers on a serving platter. Drizzle with olive oil and balsamic vinegar, then season with salt and pepper.
3. Serve immediately as a snack or appetizer.

Nutritional Information (Per Serving):
- Calories: 150 • Protein: 7g • Carbohydrates: 2g
- Fats: 12g • Fiber: 1g • Cholesterol: 15mg
- Sodium: 250mg • Potassium: 150mg • Net Carbs: 1g

These cheese and olive skewers are a quick and easy appetizer. They pair well with a glass of dry white wine or sparkling water. For added flavor, you can sprinkle the skewers with Italian seasoning or freshly grated Parmesan.

Guacamole with Pork Rinds

Prep. time: 10 min | Servings: 4
Ingredients:
- 2 ripe avocados
- 1 small red onion, finely chopped
- 1 small tomato, diced
- 1 clove garlic, minced
- 1/4 cup fresh cilantro, chopped
- Juice of 1 lime
- Salt and pepper to taste
- 1 bag pork rinds for dipping

Instructions:
1. Prepare the Guacamole: • In a medium bowl, mash the avocados with a fork until smooth. Stir in the chopped red onion, tomato, garlic, cilantro, and lime juice. Season with salt and pepper to taste.
2. Serve the guacamole with pork rinds for dipping.

Nutritional Information (Per Serving):
- Calories: 200 • Protein: 2g • Carbohydrates: 8g
- Fats: 18g • Fiber: 6g • Cholesterol: 0mg
- Sodium: 250mg • Potassium: 450mg • Net Carbs: 2g

This guacamole is perfect for dipping with pork rinds, making it a great keto-friendly snack or appetizer. Pair with a cold keto-friendly beer or a refreshing glass of iced tea.

Cauliflower Bites with Buffalo Sauce

Prep. time: 15 min | Cooking time: 25 min | Servings: 4
Ingredients:
- 1 large head of cauliflower, cut into bite-sized florets
- 2 tbsp olive oil • 1/2 tsp garlic powder
- Salt and pepper to taste

For the Buffalo Sauce: • 1/4 cup hot sauce
- 2 tbsp butter, melted • 1 tsp apple cider vinegar
- 1/2 tsp garlic powder

Instructions:
1. Preheat your oven to 400°F (200°C). Line a baking sheet with parchment paper.
2. In a large bowl, toss the cauliflower florets with olive oil, garlic powder, salt, and pepper until evenly coated. Spread the cauliflower in a single layer on the prepared baking sheet.
3. Bake in the preheated oven for 20-25 minutes, or until the cauliflower is tender and golden brown.
4. Prepare the Buffalo Sauce: • While the cauliflower is baking, whisk together the hot sauce, melted butter, apple cider vinegar, and garlic powder in a small bowl.
5. Toss the Cauliflower: • Once the cauliflower is done baking, transfer it to a large bowl. Pour the buffalo sauce over the cauliflower and toss to coat.
6. Serve immediately with a side of ranch or blue cheese dressing for dipping.

Nutritional Information (Per Serving):
- Calories: 120 • Protein: 2g • Carbohydrates: 7g
- Fats: 10g • Fiber: 3g • Cholesterol: 10mg
- Sodium: 600mg • Potassium: 300mg • Net Carbs: 4g

These buffalo cauliflower bites are a great snack or appetizer. Serve them with a side of celery sticks and keto-friendly ranch or blue cheese dressing. Pair with a cold keto-friendly beer or sparkling water.

Sausage Balls

Prep. time: 10 min | Cooking time: 20 min
Yield: 24 sausage balls

Ingredients:
- 1 lb (450g) ground sausage (mild or spicy)
- 1 cup shredded cheddar cheese
- 1/4 cup almond flour
- 1/4 cup cream cheese, softened
- 1 large egg
- 1/2 tsp garlic powder
- 1/2 tsp onion powder
- Salt and pepper to taste

Instructions:
1. Preheat your oven to 375°F (190°C). Line a baking sheet with parchment paper.
2. Prepare the Sausage Mixture: • In a large bowl, combine the ground sausage, shredded cheddar, almond flour, cream cheese, egg, garlic powder, onion powder, salt, and pepper. Mix until well combined.
3. Form the Sausage Balls: • Roll the mixture into 1-inch balls and place them on the prepared baking sheet.
4. Bake in the preheated oven for 18-20 minutes, or until the sausage balls are cooked through and golden brown.
5. Serve hot with your favorite keto-friendly dipping sauce.

Nutritional Information (Per Serving):
- Calories: 80 • Protein: 5g • Carbohydrates: 1g
- Fats: 6g • Fiber: 0g • Cholesterol: 25mg
- Sodium: 200mg • Potassium: 100mg • Net Carbs: 1g

These sausage balls are perfect for breakfast, snacks, or appetizers. Serve them with a side of keto-friendly mustard or ranch dressing. Pair with a cup of coffee or a glass of iced tea.

Chocolate Bark with Nuts

Prep. time: 10 min | Freezing time: 20 min | Servings: 8

Ingredients:
- 1 cup sugar-free dark chocolate chips
- 1/4 cup almonds, chopped
- 1/4 cup walnuts, chopped
- 1/4 cup pecans, chopped
- 1/4 tsp sea salt (optional)

Instructions:
1. Melt the Chocolate: • In a microwave-safe bowl, melt the chocolate chips in 30-second intervals, stirring in between, until fully melted and smooth.
2. Prepare the Bark: • Line a baking sheet with parchment paper. Pour the melted chocolate onto the parchment paper and spread it out evenly to about 1/4-inch thickness.
3. Add the Nuts: • Sprinkle the chopped almonds, walnuts, and pecans evenly over the melted chocolate. If desired, sprinkle a pinch of sea salt over the top.
4. Freeze: • Place the baking sheet in the freezer for about 20 minutes, or until the chocolate is fully set.
5. Once set, break the chocolate bark into pieces and serve.

Nutritional Information (Per Serving):
- Calories: 150 • Protein: 2g • Carbohydrates: 5g
- Fats: 12g • Fiber: 3g • Cholesterol: 0mg
- Sodium: 20mg • Potassium: 150mg • Net Carbs: 2g

This keto chocolate bark makes a perfect snack or dessert. Enjoy it with a cup of coffee or tea. You can also package it as a gift for a keto-friendly treat.

Desserts: Indulge Without Guilt

Yes, you can have dessert on keto—and it can be amazing! In this section, you'll find decadent, guilt-free treats that satisfy your sweet tooth without kicking you out of ketosis. From rich chocolatey delights to light and fruity favorites, these desserts prove that you don't need sugar to indulge. Perfect for special occasions or just an after-dinner treat, these recipes let you enjoy the sweet side of keto living.

Chocolate Avocado Mousse

Prep. time: 10 min | Yield: 4 servings

Ingredients:
- 2 ripe avocados
- 1/4 cup unsweetened cocoa powder
- 1/4 cup coconut milk (full-fat)
- 1/4 cup erythritol or your preferred keto sweetener
- 1 tsp vanilla extract
- Pinch of salt
- Fresh berries or keto-friendly whipped cream for topping (optional)

Instructions:

1. Prepare the Mousse: • In a blender or food processor, combine the avocados, cocoa powder, coconut milk, erythritol, vanilla extract, and salt. Blend until smooth and creamy.
2. Chill: • Spoon the mousse into individual serving bowls. Refrigerate for at least 30 minutes to allow the flavors to meld and the mousse to chill.
3. Top with fresh berries or whipped cream, if desired, and serve.

Nutritional Information (Per Serving):
- Calories: 200 • Protein: 3g • Carbohydrates: 8g
- Fats: 18g • Fiber: 5g • Cholesterol: 0mg
- Sodium: 50mg • Potassium: 600mg • Net Carbs: 3g

This mousse is rich and decadent, perfect for satisfying your chocolate cravings. Enjoy it on its own or paired with a few fresh berries for added flavor.

Almond Flour Brownies

Prep. time: 10 min | Cooking time: 25 min
Yield: 9 brownies

Ingredients:
- 1 1/2 cups almond flour
- 1/2 cup unsweetened cocoa powder
- 1/2 cup erythritol or your preferred keto sweetener
- 1/2 cup butter, melted
- 3 large eggs
- 1 tsp vanilla extract
- 1/2 tsp baking powder
- Pinch of salt
- 1/4 cup sugar-free chocolate chips (optional)

Instructions:

1. Preheat your oven to 350°F (175°C). Grease an 8x8-inch baking dish or line it with parchment paper.
2. Prepare the Batter: • In a large bowl, whisk together the almond flour, cocoa powder, erythritol, baking powder, and salt. Add the melted butter, eggs, and vanilla extract, stirring until well combined. Fold in the chocolate chips, if using.
3. Pour the batter into the prepared baking dish, spreading it out evenly. Bake in the preheated oven for 20-25 minutes, or until a toothpick inserted into the center comes out clean.
4. Allow the brownies to cool in the baking dish before slicing into squares.

Nutritional Information (Per Serving):
- Calories: 180 • Protein: 5g • Carbohydrates: 6g
- Fats: 16g • Fiber: 3g • Cholesterol: 60mg
- Sodium: 100mg • Potassium: 100mg • Net Carbs: 3g

Lemon Cheesecake Bites

Prep. time: 10 min | Chilling time: 2 hours
Yield: 12 bites

Ingredients:
- 8 oz cream cheese, softened
- 1/4 cup erythritol or your preferred keto sweetener
- 1 tbsp lemon juice
- 1 tsp lemon zest
- 1/2 tsp vanilla extract
- 1/4 cup almond flour (for crust)
- 2 tbsp butter, melted (for crust)
- 1 tbsp erythritol (for crust)

Instructions:
1. Prepare the Crust: • In a small bowl, mix together the almond flour, melted butter, and erythritol. Press the mixture into the bottom of a silicone mini muffin pan or mini cupcake liners.
2. Prepare the Filling: • In a medium bowl, beat the softened cream cheese, erythritol, lemon juice, lemon zest, and vanilla extract until smooth and creamy.
3. Assemble the Bites: • Spoon the cream cheese mixture over the crusts, filling each mold or liner. Smooth the tops with a spoon.
4. Chill: • Refrigerate for at least 2 hours, or until set.
5. Remove the cheesecake bites from the molds and serve chilled.

Nutritional Information (Per Serving):
- Calories: 100 • Protein: 2g • Carbohydrates: 2g
- Fats: 9g • Fiber: 0g • Cholesterol: 25mg
- Sodium: 60mg • Potassium: 30mg • Net Carbs: 2g

These lemon cheesecake bites are light and refreshing, perfect for a quick dessert. Enjoy them with a cup of tea or coffee.

Peanut Butter Cookies

Prep. time: 10 min | Cooking time: 15 min
Yield: 12 cookies

Ingredients:
- 1 cup peanut butter (unsweetened, no added sugar)
- 1/2 cup erythritol or your preferred keto sweetener
- 1 large egg
- 1 tsp vanilla extract
- 1/2 tsp baking powder

Instructions:
1. Preheat your oven to 350°F (175°C). Line a baking sheet with parchment paper.
2. Prepare the Dough: • In a medium bowl, mix together the peanut butter, erythritol, egg, vanilla extract, and baking powder until well combined.
3. Form the Cookies: • Roll the dough into 1-inch balls and place them on the prepared baking sheet. Flatten each ball with a fork, creating a crisscross pattern.
4. Bake in the preheated oven for 12-15 minutes, or until the edges are golden. Allow the cookies to cool on the baking sheet for a few minutes before transferring to a wire rack to cool completely.
5. Enjoy the cookies once they have cooled.

Nutritional Information (Per Serving):
- Calories: 110 • Protein: 4g • Carbohydrates: 4g
- Fats: 9g • Fiber: 1g • Cholesterol: 15mg
- Sodium: 100mg • Potassium: 130mg • Net Carbs: 3g

These keto peanut butter cookies are perfect for a quick snack or dessert. Pair them with a glass of almond milk or a cup of coffee.

Chocolate Chip Cookies

Prep. time: 10 min | Cooking time: 12 min
Yield: 12 cookies

Ingredients:
• 1 1/2 cups almond flour • 1/4 cup butter, softened
• 1/4 cup erythritol or your preferred keto sweetener
• 1 large egg • 1 tsp vanilla extract • 1/2 tsp baking powder • 1/4 tsp salt • 1/4 cup sugar-free chocolate chips

Instructions:
1. Preheat your oven to 350°F (175°C). Line a baking sheet with parchment paper.
2. Prepare the Dough: • In a large bowl, cream together the softened butter and erythritol until light and fluffy. Beat in the egg and vanilla extract until well combined.
3. Mix the Dry Ingredients: • In a separate bowl, whisk together the almond flour, baking powder, and salt. Gradually add the dry ingredients to the wet ingredients, mixing until a dough forms.
4. Gently fold the sugar-free chocolate chips into the dough.
5. Roll the dough into 1-inch balls and place them on the prepared baking sheet, spacing them about 2 inches apart. Flatten each ball slightly with your hand or the back of a spoon.
6. Bake in the preheated oven for 10-12 minutes, or until the edges are golden. Allow the cookies to cool on the baking sheet for a few minutes before transferring to a wire rack to cool completely.

Nutritional Information (Per Serving):
• Calories: 120 • Protein: 3g • Carbohydrates: 4g
• Fats: 10g • Fiber: 2g • Cholesterol: 20mg
• Sodium: 90mg • Potassium: 50mg • Net Carbs: 2g

Raspberry Swirl Cheesecake

Prep. time: 20 min | Cook. time: 50 min | Chilling: 2 hrs

Ingredients:
For the Crust: • 1 cup almond flour • 2 tbsp erythritol or your preferred keto sweetener • 3 tbsp butter, melted
For the Filling: • 16 oz (450g) cream cheese, softened
• 1/2 cup erythritol or your preferred keto sweetener
• 2 large eggs • 1 tsp vanilla extract • 1/4 cup heavy cream
For the Raspberry Swirl: • 1/2 cup fresh or frozen raspberries • 2 tbsp erythritol or your preferred keto sweetener

Instructions:
1. Preheat your oven to 325°F (160°C). Grease a 9-inch springform pan or line it with parchment paper.
2. Prepare the Crust: • In a small bowl, mix together the almond flour, erythritol, and melted butter until the mixture resembles wet sand. Press the mixture into the bottom of the prepared springform pan. Bake the crust for 8-10 minutes, or until lightly golden. Remove from the oven and set aside to cool.
3. Prepare the Filling: • In a large bowl, beat the cream cheese and erythritol until smooth and creamy. Add the eggs, one at a time, beating well after each addition. Stir in the vanilla extract and heavy cream until fully combined.
4. Prepare the Raspberry Swirl: • In a small saucepan, combine the raspberries and erythritol. Cook over medium heat until the raspberries break down and the mixture thickens slightly, about 5 minutes. Strain the mixture through a fine-mesh sieve to remove the seeds.
5. Assemble the Cheesecake: • Pour the cream cheese filling over the cooled crust. Spoon the raspberry sauce over the filling and use a knife or skewer to swirl the sauce into the filling, creating a marbled effect.
6. Bake the cheesecake in the preheated oven for 45-50 minutes, or until the center is set and the edges are lightly golden. Turn off the oven and leave the cheesecake inside with the door slightly ajar for 1 hour. Refrigerate the cheesecake for at least 2 hours, or until fully chilled.

Nutritional Information (Per Serving):
• Calories: 320
• Protein: 6g
• Carbohydrates: 6g
• Fats: 30g
• Fiber: 2g
• Cholesterol: 110mg
• Sodium: 200mg
• Potassium: 100mg
• Net Carbs: 4g

Cinnamon Rolls

Prep. time: 20 min | Cooking time: 20 min
Chilling time: 30 min | Yield: 8 rolls

Ingredients:
- 2 cups mozzarella cheese, shredded
- 2 oz cream cheese • 1 1/4 cups almond flour
- 1 tbsp erythritol or your preferred keto sweetener
- 1 tsp baking powder • 1 large egg

For the Filling: • 1/4 cup butter, melted
- 2 tbsp erythritol or your preferred keto sweetener
- 1 tbsp ground cinnamon

For the Frosting: • 2 oz cream cheese, softened
- 2 tbsp butter, softened • 1/4 cup powdered erythritol
- 1/2 tsp vanilla extract

Instructions:
1. In a microwave-safe bowl, combine the mozzarella cheese and cream cheese. Microwave on high for 1 minute, then stir until smooth. If necessary, microwave for an additional 30 seconds until fully melted and combined • In a separate bowl, whisk together the almond flour, erythritol, and baking powder. Add the dry ingredients to the melted cheese mixture, along with the egg. Mix until a dough forms.
2. Chill the Dough: • Cover the dough with plastic wrap and refrigerate for 30 minutes to firm up.
3. Prepare the Filling: • In a small bowl, mix together the melted butter, erythritol, and cinnamon.
4. Preheat your oven to 350°F (175°C). Roll the chilled dough between two sheets of parchment paper into a rectangle about 1/4 inch thick. Spread the cinnamon filling evenly over the dough.
5. Carefully roll the dough into a log, starting from one long side. Slice the log into 8 even pieces and place the rolls in a greased 9-inch baking dish.
6. Bake in the preheated oven for 18-20 minutes, or until the rolls are golden brown and cooked through.
7. While the rolls are baking, prepare the frosting. In a small bowl, beat together the softened cream cheese, butter, powdered erythritol, and vanilla extract until smooth and creamy. Spread the frosting over the warm cinnamon rolls and serve.

Nutritional Information (Per Roll):
- Calories: 250
- Protein: 10g
- Carbohydrates: 5g
- Fats: 22g
- Fiber: 2g
- Cholesterol: 70mg
- Sodium: 250mg
- Potassium: 100mg
- Net Carbs: 3g

Coconut Flour Cupcakes with Frosting

Prep. time: 15min | Cooking time: 20 min
Yield: 12 cupcakes

Ingredients:
- 1/2 cup coconut flour • 1/2 cup butter, melted
- 1/2 cup erythritol or your preferred keto sweetener
- 6 large eggs • 1/2 cup almond milk • 1 tsp vanilla extract • 1/2 tsp baking powder • 1/4 tsp salt

For the Frosting: • 1/2 cup butter, softened • 4 oz cream cheese, softened • 1/4 cup powdered erythritol
- 1 tsp vanilla extract

Instructions:
1. Preheat your oven to 350°F (175°C). Line a muffin tin with cupcake liners.
2. Prepare the Batter: • In a large bowl, whisk together the coconut flour, erythritol, baking powder, and salt. Add the melted butter, eggs, almond milk, and vanilla extract, mixing until smooth and well combined.
3. Divide the batter evenly among the cupcake liners, filling each about 2/3 full. Bake in the preheated oven for 18-20 minutes, or until a toothpick inserted into the center comes out clean.
4. Allow the cupcakes to cool in the tin for 5 minutes, then transfer to a wire rack to cool completely.
5. Prepare the Frosting: • In a medium bowl, beat together the softened butter, cream cheese, powdered erythritol, and vanilla extract until smooth and creamy.
6. Once the cupcakes are completely cool, spread or pipe the frosting onto each cupcake. Serve immediately.

Nutritional Information (Per Cupcake):
- Calories: 200 • Protein: 4g • Carbohydrates: 5g
- Fats: 18g • Fiber: 3g • Cholesterol: 80mg
- Sodium: 150mg • Potassium: 60mg • Net Carbs: 2g

Chocolate Coconut Fat Bombs

Prep. time: 10 min | Freezing time: 30 min
Yield: 12 fat bombs

Ingredients:
- 1/2 cup coconut oil, melted
- 1/2 cup unsweetened shredded coconut
- 1/4 cup unsweetened cocoa powder
- 1/4 cup almond butter
- 2 tbsp erythritol or your preferred keto sweetener
- 1/2 tsp vanilla extract
- Pinch of salt

Instructions:
1. Prepare the Mixture: • In a medium bowl, combine the melted coconut oil, shredded coconut, cocoa powder, almond butter, erythritol, vanilla extract, and salt. Mix until smooth and well combined.
2. Form the Fat Bombs: • Pour the mixture into silicone molds or mini muffin liners. Freeze for at least 30 minutes, or until solid.
3. Once frozen, remove the fat bombs from the molds and store them in an airtight container in the freezer. Serve chilled.

Nutritional Information (Per Serving):
- Calories: 120 • Protein: 1g • Carbohydrates: 3g
- Fats: 12g • Fiber: 2g • Cholesterol: 0mg
- Sodium: 10mg • Potassium: 50mg • Net Carbs: 1g

These chocolate coconut fat bombs are perfect for a quick snack or dessert. Enjoy them with a cup of hot coffee or tea for a satisfying keto treat.

Tiramisu with Mascarpone

Prep. time: 20 min | Chilling time: 4 hours
Yield: 6 servings

Ingredients:

For the Ladyfingers: • 3/4 cup almond flour • 1/4 cup coconut flour • 1/4 cup erythritol • 1/2 tsp baking powder • 1/4 tsp salt • 3 large eggs • 1/4 cup butter, melted • 1 tsp vanilla extract

For the Mascarpone Cream: • 8 oz mascarpone cheese • 1/2 cup heavy cream • 2 tbsp powdered erythritol • 1 tsp vanilla extract

For the Coffee Mixture: • 1/2 cup strong brewed coffee • 1 tbsp erythritol • 1 tbsp dark rum (optional)

For Dusting: • 1 tbsp unsweetened cocoa powder

Instructions:
1. Preheat your oven to 350°F (175°C). Line a baking sheet with parchment paper • In a medium bowl, whisk together the almond flour, coconut flour, erythritol, baking powder, and salt. In a separate bowl, beat the eggs, melted butter, and vanilla extract. Combine the wet and dry ingredients to form a thick batter • Spoon the batter into a piping bag and pipe 3-inch long ladyfingers onto the prepared baking sheet. Bake for 10-12 minutes, or until golden. Allow the ladyfingers to cool completely.
2. Prepare the Mascarpone Cream: • In a large bowl, beat together the mascarpone cheese, heavy cream, powdered erythritol, and vanilla extract until smooth and creamy.
3. Prepare the Coffee Mixture: • In a shallow dish, combine the brewed coffee, erythritol, and dark rum (if using).
4. Quickly dip each ladyfinger into the coffee mixture and arrange a layer in the bottom of a 9x9-inch dish. Spread half of the mascarpone cream over the ladyfingers. Repeat with another layer of soaked ladyfingers and the remaining cream.
5. Cover the tiramisu and refrigerate for at least 4 hours, or overnight, to allow the flavors to meld. Dust the top with unsweetened cocoa powder before serving.

Nutritional Information (Per Serving):
- Calories: 350
- Protein: 7g
- Carbohydrates: 6g
- Fats: 33g
- Fiber: 3g
- Cholesterol: 140mg
- Sodium: 150mg
- Potassium: 120mg
- Net Carbs: 3g

Pumpkin Spice Muffins

Prep. time: 15 min | Cooking time: 20 min
Yield: 12 muffins

Ingredients:
- 1 1/2 cups almond flour • 1/4 cup coconut flour
- 1/2 cup erythritol or your preferred keto sweetener
- 1 tsp baking powder • 1/2 tsp baking soda • 1/4 tsp salt
- 2 tsp pumpkin pie spice • 3/4 cup pumpkin puree (unsweetened) • 3 large eggs • 1/4 cup coconut oil, melted • 1 tsp vanilla extract

Instructions:
1. Preheat your oven to 350°F (175°C). Line a muffin tin with cupcake liners.
2. Prepare the Batter: • In a large bowl, whisk together the almond flour, coconut flour, erythritol, baking powder, baking soda, salt, and pumpkin pie spice. In a separate bowl, whisk together the pumpkin puree, eggs, melted coconut oil, and vanilla extract until smooth
• Gradually add the wet ingredients to the dry ingredients, mixing until just combined. Do not overmix.
3. Divide the batter evenly among the muffin liners, filling each about 2/3 full. Bake in the preheated oven for 18-20 minutes, or until a toothpick inserted into the center comes out clean.
4. Allow the muffins to cool in the tin for 5 minutes, then transfer to a wire rack to cool completely.

Nutritional Information (Per Muffin):
- Calories: 140 • Protein: 5g • Carbohydrates: 6g
- Fats: 11g • Fiber: 3g • Cholesterol: 45mg
- Sodium: 150mg • Potassium: 100mg • Net Carbs: 3g

These pumpkin spice muffins are perfect for a cozy fall treat. Pair them with a cup of hot coffee or tea, and consider topping them with a dollop of keto-friendly cream cheese frosting.

Keto Pecan Pie

Prep. time: 20 min | Cooking time: 35 min
Yield: 8 servings

Ingredients:
For the Crust: • 1 1/2 cups almond flour
• 1/4 cup coconut flour • 1/4 cup erythritol or your preferred keto sweetener • 1/4 cup butter, melted
• 1 large egg • 1/2 tsp vanilla extract • Pinch of salt
For the Filling: • 1 1/2 cups pecan halves • 3 large eggs
• 3/4 cup erythritol or your preferred keto sweetener
• 1/4 cup butter, melted • 1/2 cup sugar-free maple syrup • 1 tsp vanilla extract • 1/2 tsp salt

Instructions:
1. Preheat your oven to 350°F (175°C). Grease a 9-inch pie dish or line it with parchment paper.
2. In a large bowl, combine the almond flour, coconut flour, erythritol, melted butter, egg, vanilla extract, and salt. Mix until a dough forms. Press the dough into the bottom and up the sides of the prepared pie dish. Prick the bottom with a fork • Bake the crust in the preheated oven for 10 minutes, or until lightly golden. Remove from the oven and set aside to cool.
3. In a large bowl, whisk together the eggs, erythritol, melted butter, sugar-free maple syrup, vanilla extract, and salt until smooth. Stir in the pecan halves.
4. Pour the filling into the pre-baked crust, spreading the pecans evenly.
5. Bake in the preheated oven for 25-30 minutes, or until the filling is set and the top is golden. If the crust starts to brown too quickly, cover the edges with foil.

Nutritional Information (Per Serving):
- Calories: 350 • Protein: 7g • Carbohydrates: 8g
- Fats: 32g • Fiber: 4g • Cholesterol: 85mg
- Sodium: 180mg • Potassium: 150mg • Net Carbs: 4g

Chocolate Fudge

Prep. time: 10 min | Chilling time: 2 hours
Yield: 16 pieces

Ingredients:
- 1/2 cup coconut oil
- 1/2 cup almond butter
- 1/2 cup unsweetened cocoa powder
- 1/4 cup erythritol or your preferred keto sweetener
- 1/2 tsp vanilla extract
- Pinch of salt
- 1/4 cup chopped nuts (optional)

Instructions:
1. Prepare the Mixture: • In a medium saucepan over low heat, combine the coconut oil, almond butter, cocoa powder, erythritol, vanilla extract, and salt. Stir continuously until the mixture is smooth and well combined. If using, stir in the chopped nuts.
2. Chill: • Pour the mixture into a small, square dish lined with parchment paper. Smooth the top with a spatula. Refrigerate for at least 2 hours, or until firm.
3. Once set, lift the fudge out of the dish using the parchment paper. Cut into 16 squares and serve chilled.

Nutritional Information (Per Piece):
- Calories: 120 • Protein: 2g • Carbohydrates: 3g
- Fats: 12g • Fiber: 2g • Cholesterol: 0mg
- Sodium: 10mg • Potassium: 80mg • Net Carbs: 1g

This keto chocolate fudge is rich, creamy, and perfect for satisfying chocolate cravings. Store in the refrigerator and enjoy as a quick treat or dessert.

Key Lime Pie

Prep. time: 15 min | Cooking time: 15 min
Chilling time: 2 hours | Yield: 8 servings

Ingredients:
- 1 1/2 cups almond flour • 2 tbsp erythritol or your preferred keto sweetener • 1/4 cup butter, melted
- 1/2 tsp vanilla extract

For the Filling:
- 1/2 cup fresh lime juice (about 4-5 limes) • 2 tbsp lime zest • 1/2 cup erythritol or your preferred keto sweetener • 3 large egg yolks • 1/2 cup heavy cream • 1/4 cup cream cheese, softened • 1/2 tsp vanilla extract

Instructions:
1. Preheat your oven to 350°F (175°C). Grease a 9-inch pie dish or tart pan.
2. In a medium bowl, combine the almond flour, erythritol, melted butter, and vanilla extract. Press the mixture into the bottom and up the sides of the prepared pie dish. Bake for 10 minutes, or until lightly golden. Remove from the oven and set aside to cool.
3. In a medium bowl, whisk together the lime juice, lime zest, erythritol, egg yolks, heavy cream, cream cheese, and vanilla extract until smooth and well combined.
4. Assemble the Pie: • Pour the filling into the pre-baked crust. Bake in the preheated oven for 12-15 minutes, or until the filling is set but still slightly jiggly in the center.
5. Allow the pie to cool to room temperature, then refrigerate for at least 2 hours, or until fully chilled.
6. Slice the pie and serve with a dollop of keto-friendly whipped cream and a sprinkle of lime zest.

Nutritional Information (Per Serving):
- Calories: 260 • Protein: 6g • Carbohydrates: 5g
- Fats: 24g • Fiber: 3g • Cholesterol: 120mg
- Sodium: 70mg • Potassium: 100mg • Net Carbs: 2g

Butter Pecan Ice Cream

Prep. time: 10 min | Cooking time: 10 min
Churning time: 20 min | Freezing time: 2 hours
Yield: 4 servings

Ingredients:
- 1/2 cup pecans, chopped • 1 tbsp butter
- 1 1/2 cups heavy cream • 1/2 cup unsweetened almond milk • 1/3 cup erythritol or your preferred keto sweetener • 1 tsp vanilla extract • Pinch of salt

Instructions:
1. In a small skillet, melt the butter over medium heat. Add the chopped pecans and toast until golden brown and fragrant, about 5 minutes. Set aside to cool.
2. In a medium saucepan, combine the heavy cream, almond milk, erythritol, vanilla extract, and salt. Heat over medium-low heat, stirring occasionally, until the mixture is warm and the erythritol is dissolved. Do not let it boil.
3. Remove the cream mixture from the heat and allow it to cool to room temperature. Stir in the toasted pecans. Cover and refrigerate for at least 2 hours, or until thoroughly chilled.
4. Churn the Ice Cream: • Pour the chilled mixture into an ice cream maker and churn according to the manufacturer's instructions, usually about 20 minutes, until the mixture thickens and resembles soft-serve ice cream.
5. Transfer the churned ice cream to an airtight container and freeze for at least 2 hours, or until firm.
6. Scoop the ice cream into bowls and serve.

Nutritional Information (Per Serving):
- Calories: 350 • Protein: 3g • Carbohydrates: 5g
- Fats: 34g • Fiber: 2g • Cholesterol: 110mg
- Sodium: 60mg • Potassium: 100mg • Net Carbs: 3g

Cheesecake with Almond Crust

Prep. time: 15 min | Cooking time: 15 min
Chilling time: 2 hours | Yield: 8 servings

Ingredients:
- 1 1/2 cups almond flour • 2 tbsp erythritol or your preferred keto sweetener • 1/4 cup butter, melted
- 1/2 tsp vanilla extract

For the Filling:
- 1/2 cup fresh lime juice (about 4-5 limes)
- 2 tbsp lime zest • 1/2 cup erythritol or your preferred keto sweetener • 3 large egg yolks • 1/2 cup heavy cream
- 1/4 cup cream cheese, softened • 1/2 tsp vanilla extract

Instructions:
1. Preheat your oven to 350°F (175°C). Grease a 9-inch pie dish or tart pan.
2. In a medium bowl, combine the almond flour, erythritol, melted butter, and vanilla extract. Press the mixture into the bottom and up the sides of the prepared pie dish. Bake for 10 minutes, or until lightly golden. Remove from the oven and set aside to cool.
3. In a medium bowl, whisk together the lime juice, lime zest, erythritol, egg yolks, heavy cream, cream cheese, and vanilla extract until smooth and well combined.
4. Assemble the Pie: • Pour the filling into the pre-baked crust. Bake in the preheated oven for 12-15 minutes, or until the filling is set but still slightly jiggly in the center.
5. Allow the pie to cool to room temperature, then refrigerate for at least 2 hours, or until fully chilled.
6. Slice the pie and serve with a dollop of keto-friendly whipped cream and a sprinkle of lime zest.

Nutritional Information (Per Serving):
- Calories: 260 • Protein: 6g • Carbohydrates: 5g
- Fats: 24g • Fiber: 3g • Cholesterol: 120mg
- Sodium: 70mg • Potassium: 100mg • Net Carbs: 2g

Lemon Bars

Prep. time: 15 min | Cooking time: 30 min
Chilling time: 1 hour | Yield: 12 bars

Ingredients:
For the Crust: • 1 1/2 cups almond flour • 2 tbsp erythritol or your preferred keto sweetener • 1/4 cup butter, melted
For the Lemon Filling: • 3 large eggs • 3/4 cup erythritol or your preferred keto sweetener • 1/2 cup fresh lemon juice (about 4 lemons) • 2 tbsp lemon zest
• 2 tbsp coconut flour • Pinch of salt

Instructions:
1. Preheat your oven to 350°F (175°C). Line an 8x8-inch baking dish with parchment paper.
2. Prepare the Crust: • In a medium bowl, mix together the almond flour, erythritol, and melted butter until the mixture resembles wet sand. Press the mixture firmly into the bottom of the prepared baking dish. Bake for 10 minutes, or until lightly golden. Remove from the oven and set aside to cool.
3. Prepare the Lemon Filling: • In a large bowl, whisk together the eggs, erythritol, lemon juice, lemon zest, coconut flour, and salt until smooth and well combined.
4. Assemble the Bars: • Pour the lemon filling over the pre-baked crust, spreading it out evenly.
5. Bake in the preheated oven for 18-20 minutes, or until the filling is set and just starting to turn golden around the edges.
6. Allow the lemon bars to cool to room temperature, then refrigerate for at least 1 hour, or until fully chilled.
7. Cut into squares and serve chilled.

Nutritional Information (Per Serving):
• Calories: 150 • Protein: 4g • Carbohydrates: 6g
• Fats: 13g • Fiber: 2g • Cholesterol: 70mg
• Sodium: 60mg • Potassium: 50mg • Net Carbs: 4g

Chocolate Covered Almonds

Prep. time: 10 min | Chilling time: 30 min
Yield: 8 servings

Ingredients:
• 1 cup raw almonds
• 1/2 cup sugar-free dark chocolate chips
• 1 tbsp coconut oil
• Pinch of sea salt (optional)

Instructions:
1. Melt the Chocolate: • In a microwave-safe bowl, combine the dark chocolate chips and coconut oil. Microwave in 30-second intervals, stirring in between, until the chocolate is fully melted and smooth.
2. Coat the Almonds: • Add the almonds to the melted chocolate, stirring until all the almonds are fully coated.
3. Chill: • Using a fork, lift each almond out of the chocolate, allowing any excess chocolate to drip off, and place them on a parchment-lined baking sheet. If desired, sprinkle the almonds with a pinch of sea salt. Refrigerate for at least 30 minutes, or until the chocolate is set.
4. Once the chocolate is firm, transfer the chocolate-covered almonds to an airtight container and store in the refrigerator until ready to serve.

Nutritional Information (Per Serving):
• Calories: 170 • Protein: 4g • Carbohydrates: 6g
• Fats: 15g • Fiber: 4g • Cholesterol: 0mg
• Sodium: 5mg • Potassium: 150mg • Net Carbs: 2g

These chocolate-covered almonds are a simple yet satisfying keto snack or dessert. Enjoy them on their own or as part of a keto-friendly trail mix.

Unique Recipe Categories with Flexible Plan System

Welcome to a world of delicious variety within the keto lifestyle! In this chapter, we're diving into unique recipe categories that add flexibility, flavor, and fun to your meals. While the core recipes introduced earlier provide the essentials for daily keto eating, this chapter expands on them with recipes designed to meet specific needs, tastes, and occasions.

Whether you're short on time, looking to impress at weekend gatherings, or aiming to stick to a budget, these unique categories have you covered. You'll find quick weekday meals that fit seamlessly into a busy schedule, family-friendly dishes that everyone will love, and meal-prep options that simplify your weekly planning. For special occasions, there are holiday-themed recipes, and if you're craving international flavors, you'll enjoy recipes that bring a world of taste to your keto journey.

Each section in this chapter offers a selection of recipes tailored to specific lifestyles and preferences, giving you the flexibility to adapt keto to fit your life. As you explore these recipes, remember that keto can be as diverse and enjoyable as any other way of eating. From everyday favorites to adventurous new flavors, let this chapter inspire you to make keto your own and bring creativity to every meal.

Quick Weekday Meals

Shrimp Stir-Fry with Bell Peppers

Ingredients:
- 1 tbsp olive oil
- 1/2 lb shrimp, peeled and deveined
- 1 bell pepper, thinly sliced (any color)
- 1/2 small onion, thinly sliced
- 1 clove garlic, minced
- Salt and pepper to taste
- 1/2 tsp red pepper flakes (optional)
- 1 tbsp soy sauce or coconut aminos

Servings: 2 **Prep Time:** 5 minutes
Cook Time: 10 minutes

Instructions:
- Heat the olive oil in a skillet over medium-high heat.
- Add the onion and bell pepper, sauté for 3-4 minutes until tender.
- Add the garlic, shrimp, salt, pepper, and red pepper flakes, if using. Cook for 3-4 minutes, until the shrimp are pink and cooked through.
- Stir in the soy sauce or coconut aminos and serve immediately.

Nutritional Information (per serving):
Calories: 180, Protein: 22g, Carbs: 4g, Fat: 9g, Fiber: 1g

Turkey and Spinach Stuffed Portobello Mushrooms

Ingredients:
- 4 large portobello mushrooms, stems removed
- 1/2 lb ground turkey
- 1 cup fresh spinach, chopped
- 1/2 cup mozzarella cheese, shredded
- 1 tbsp olive oil
- 1 clove garlic, minced
- Salt and pepper to taste

Servings: 2 **Prep Time:** 10 minutes
Cook Time: 20 minutes

Instructions:
- Preheat oven to 375°F (190°C).
- In a skillet, heat olive oil and sauté garlic until fragrant. Add ground turkey and cook until browned. Stir in spinach and cook until wilted.
- Stuff the turkey and spinach mixture into the mushroom caps, top with mozzarella cheese, and bake for 15 minutes or until cheese is melted and bubbly.

Nutritional Information (per serving):
Calories: 290, Protein: 30g, Carbs: 8g, Fat: 17g, Fiber: 3g, Sodium: 460mg, Potassium: 840mg

63

Quick Weekday Meals · Unique Recipe Categories with Flexible Plan System

Sausage and Kale Skillet

Ingredients:
- 1 tbsp olive oil
- 2 sausage links (keto-friendly), sliced
- 1 cup kale, chopped
- 1 clove garlic, minced
- Salt and pepper to taste
- 1 tbsp grated Parmesan cheese (optional)

Servings: 2 **Prep Time:** 5 minutes **Cook Time:** 10 minutes

Instructions:
- In a skillet over medium heat, warm the olive oil.
- Add the sausage slices and cook until browned, about 3-4 minutes.
- Add the kale and garlic, season with salt and pepper, and cook until the kale is wilted, about 3 minutes.
- Sprinkle with Parmesan cheese if desired, and serve warm.

Nutritional Information (per serving): Calories: 210, Protein: 16g, Carbs: 5g, Fat: 14g, Fiber: 2g

Chicken Fajita Bowl

Ingredients:
- 2 chicken breasts, sliced
- 1 red bell pepper, sliced
- 1 green bell pepper, sliced
- 1 small onion, sliced
- 2 tbsp olive oil
- 1 tsp paprika
- 1 tsp cumin
- Salt and pepper to taste
- 1 avocado, sliced
- 1 cup cauliflower rice, cooked
- 2 tbsp sour cream (optional)

Servings: 2 **Prep Time:** 10 minutes **Cook Time:** 15 minutes

Instructions:
- Heat olive oil in a skillet over medium heat. Add chicken, season with paprika, cumin, salt, and pepper, and cook until browned, about 8-10 minutes.
- Add bell peppers and onions, and sauté until vegetables are tender.
- Serve the chicken and vegetables over cauliflower rice, topped with sliced avocado and sour cream if desired.

Nutritional Information (per serving): Calories: 320, Protein: 25g, Carbs: 7g, Fat: 22g, Fiber: 5g, Sodium: 380mg, Potassium: 810mg

Eggplant Stir-Fry

Ingredients:
- 1 medium eggplant, diced
- 1/2 lb ground pork
- 1 tbsp soy sauce (or tamari for gluten-free)
- 1 tbsp olive oil
- 2 cloves garlic, minced
- 1/2 tsp ground ginger
- 1 green onion, chopped for garnish

Servings: 2 **Prep Time:** 10 minutes **Cook Time:** 15 minutes

Instructions:
- Heat olive oil in a skillet over medium heat. Add ground pork and cook until browned.
- Add diced eggplant, garlic, and ginger, and stir-fry for 8-10 minutes until the eggplant is tender.
- Stir in soy sauce, cook for another 2 minutes, and garnish with chopped green onion.

Nutritional Information (per serving): Calories: 260, Protein: 18g, Carbs: 10g, Fat: 18g, Fiber: 4g, Sodium: 650mg, Potassium: 620mg

Quick Weekday Meals Unique Recipe Categories with Flexible Plan System

Grilled Pork Chops with Herb Butter

Ingredients:
- 2 boneless pork chops
- 2 tbsp olive oil
- Salt and pepper to taste
- 2 tbsp butter, softened
- 1 tsp fresh parsley, chopped
- 1 tsp fresh thyme, chopped

Servings: 2 **Prep Time:** 10 minutes
Cook Time: 12 minutes

Instructions:
- Rub pork chops with olive oil, salt, and pepper.
- Preheat grill to medium heat and grill pork chops for 5-6 minutes per side until fully cooked.
- In a small bowl, mix softened butter with parsley and thyme. Serve the pork chops topped with herb butter.

Nutritional Information (per serving):
Calories: 320, Protein: 27g, Carbs: 1g, Fat: 24g, Fiber: 0g, Sodium: 370mg, Potassium: 480mg

Zucchini and Ham Roll-Ups

Ingredients:
- 2 medium zucchinis, thinly sliced lengthwise
- 4 slices of ham
- 1/2 cup mozzarella cheese, shredded
- 1 tbsp olive oil
- Salt and pepper to taste

Servings: 2 **Prep Time:** 10 minutes
Cook Time: 15 minutes

Instructions:
- Preheat oven to 375°F (190°C).
- Lay out the zucchini slices and top each with a slice of ham and some mozzarella cheese.
- Roll up each slice and place them seam-side down in a baking dish. Drizzle with olive oil and season with salt and pepper.
- Bake for 15 minutes until the cheese is melted and bubbly.

Nutritional Information (per serving):
Calories: 240, Protein: 18g, Carbs: 4g, Fat: 17g, Fiber: 1g, Sodium: 620mg, Potassium: 520mg

Avocado and Bacon Salad

Ingredients:
- 1 large avocado, diced
- 4 slices of bacon, cooked and crumbled
- 1 cup mixed greens
- 1 tbsp olive oil
- 1 tsp lemon juice
- Salt and pepper to taste

Servings: 2 **Prep Time:** 10 minutes
Cook Time: 5 minutes

Instructions:
- In a bowl, combine diced avocado, crumbled bacon, and mixed greens.
- Drizzle with olive oil and lemon juice, season with salt and pepper, and toss to coat.

Nutritional Information (per serving):
Calories: 310, Protein: 8g, Carbs: 5g, Fat: 18g, Fiber: 4g, Sodium: 420mg, Potassium: 550mg

Quick Weekday Meals · Unique Recipe Categories with Flexible Plan System

Chicken Piccata with Zoodles

Ingredients:
- 2 chicken breasts, pounded thin
- 1/4 cup almond flour
- 2 tbsp olive oil
- 1/4 cup chicken broth
- 2 tbsp lemon juice
- 1 tbsp capers
- 1 zucchini, spiralized into noodles

Servings: 2 **Prep Time:** 10 minutes **Cook Time:** 15 minutes

Instructions:
- Dredge the chicken breasts in almond flour.
- Heat olive oil in a skillet over medium heat and cook the chicken until browned on both sides.
- Add chicken broth, lemon juice, and capers, simmer for 5 minutes. Serve over zucchini noodles.

Nutritional Information (per serving):
Calories: 330, Protein: 28g, Carbs: 6g, Fat: 22g, Fiber: 3g, Sodium: 550mg, Potassium: 680mg

Greek Salad with Feta and Olives

Ingredients:
- 1 cucumber, diced
- 1/2 cup cherry tomatoes, halved
- 1/4 cup Kalamata olives, sliced
- 1/4 cup feta cheese, crumbled
- 1 tbsp olive oil
- 1 tsp red wine vinegar
- Salt and pepper to taste

Servings: 2 **Prep Time:** 10 minutes

Instructions:
- Combine cucumber, cherry tomatoes, olives, and feta in a bowl.
- Drizzle with olive oil and red wine vinegar, season with salt and pepper, and toss.

Nutritional Information (per serving):
Calories: 220, Protein: 5g, Carbs: 6g, Fat: 20g, Fiber: 2g, Sodium: 460mg, Potassium: 380mg

Pork Stir-Fry with Bok Choy

Ingredients:
- 1/2 lb pork tenderloin, sliced thin
- 1 tbsp soy sauce (or tamari for gluten-free)
- 1 tbsp olive oil
- 2 cloves garlic, minced
- 1 head bok choy, chopped

Servings: 2 **Prep Time:** 10 minutes **Cook Time:** 15 minutes

Instructions:
- Heat olive oil in a skillet over medium heat. Add pork slices and cook until browned.
- Add garlic and bok choy, stir-frying until bok choy is wilted and tender. Stir in soy sauce and cook for another minute.

Nutritional Information (per serving):
Calories: 240, Protein: 22g, Carbs: 6g, Fat: 15g, Fiber: 2g, Sodium: 650mg, Potassium: 620mg

Weekend Feasts

Unique Recipe Categories with Flexible Plan System

Lamb Shanks with Garlic and Rosemary

Ingredients:
- 2 lamb shanks
- 1 tbsp olive oil
- 2 cloves garlic, minced
- 1 sprig rosemary
- 1 cup beef broth
- Salt and pepper to taste

Servings: 2 **Prep Time:** 15 minutes
Cook Time: 1 hour 30 minutes

Instructions:
- Preheat oven to 350°F (175°C). Season the lamb shanks with salt and pepper.
- In a large oven-safe pot, heat olive oil and brown the lamb shanks on all sides.
- Add garlic, rosemary, and beef broth to the pot. Cover and transfer to the oven, cooking for 1.5 hours until the meat is tender.

Nutritional Information (per serving):
Calories: 600, Protein: 46g, Carbs: 3g, Fat: 44g, Fiber: 1g, Sodium: 500mg, Potassium: 720mg

Chicken Cordon Bleu

Ingredients:
- 2 chicken breasts, pounded thin
- 2 slices of ham
- 2 slices of Swiss cheese
- 1/2 cup almond flour
- 1 egg, beaten
- 1 tbsp olive oil

Servings: 2 **Prep Time:** 15 minutes
Cook Time: 25 minutes

Instructions:
- Preheat oven to 375°F (190°C). Place a slice of ham and cheese on each chicken breast and roll them up.
- Dip each chicken roll in the beaten egg and coat with almond flour.
- Heat olive oil in a skillet and sear the chicken rolls until golden, about 3 minutes per side.
- Transfer to the oven and bake for 20 min.

Nutritional Information (per serving):
Calories: 380, Protein: 38g, Carbs: 4g, Fat: 24g, Fiber: 2g, Sodium: 820mg, Potassium: 620mg

Ribeye Steak with Creamy Peppercorn Sauce

Ingredients:
- 2 ribeye steaks (6 oz each)
- 1 tbsp olive oil
- 1/2 cup heavy cream
- 1 tsp black peppercorns, crushed
- Salt to taste

Servings: 2 **Prep Time:** 5 minutes
Cook Time: 10 minutes

Instructions:
- Heat olive oil in a skillet over high heat. Sear the steaks for 3-4 minutes on each side, depending on preferred doneness.
- Remove steaks and set aside. In the same skillet, reduce heat to medium and add cream and crushed peppercorns. Simmer until thickened.
- Pour the peppercorn sauce over the steaks before serving.

Nutritional Information (per serving):
Calories: 620, Protein: 45g, Carbs: 2g, Fat: 48g, Fiber: 0g, Sodium: 320mg, Potassium: 680mg

Weekend Feasts

Unique Recipe Categories with Flexible Plan System

Crab-Stuffed Mushrooms

Ingredients:
- 6 large mushrooms, stems removed
- 1/2 cup crab meat
- 2 tbsp cream cheese
- 2 tbsp Parmesan cheese, grated
- 1 tbsp fresh parsley, chopped

Instructions:
- Preheat oven to 375°F (190°C). In a bowl, mix crab meat, cream cheese, Parmesan, and parsley.
- Stuff the mushroom caps with the crab mixture and place on a baking sheet.
- Bake for 12-15 minutes until the mushrooms are tender and the tops are golden.

Nutritional Information (per serving):
Calories: 210, Protein: 18g, Carbs: 4g, Fat: 14g, Fiber: 1g, Sodium: 320mg, Potassium: 440mg

Servings: 2 **Prep Time:** 10 minutes
Cook Time: 15 minutes

Roasted Duck with Orange Glaze

Ingredients:
- 1 whole duck (about 4 lbs)
- 1/4 cup butter, melted
- 1/4 cup orange zest
- 2 tbsp balsamic vinegar
- 2 tbsp soy sauce (or coconut aminos)
- Salt and pepper to taste

Instructions:
- Preheat the oven to 400°F (200°C).
- Season the duck with salt and pepper. Roast in the oven for 1 hour, basting with butter every 15 minutes.
- Mix the orange zest, balsamic vinegar, and soy sauce. Brush over the duck in the final 10 minutes of cooking.

Nutritional Information (per serving):
Calories: 600, Protein: 40g, Carbs: 4g, Fat: 45g, Fiber: 1g, Sodium: 300mg, Potassium: 420mg

Servings: 4 **Prep Time:** 15 minutes
Cook Time: 1 hour

Surf and Turf with Garlic Butter

Ingredients:
- 2 beef steaks (4 oz each)
- 6 large shrimp, peeled
- 2 tbsp butter, melted
- 1 clove garlic, minced
- 1 tbsp olive oil
- Salt and pepper to taste

Instructions:
- Heat olive oil in a skillet over medium heat. Season steaks with salt and pepper and sear for 3-4 minutes per side.
- In another skillet, melt butter and sauté shrimp with garlic for 3-4 minutes until pink.
- Serve the steak with shrimp, drizzling garlic butter on top.

Nutritional Information (per serving):
Calories: 450, Protein: 36g, Carbs: 2g, Fat: 32g, Fiber: 0g, Sodium: 540mg, Potassium: 710mg

Servings: 2 **Prep Time:** 10 minutes
Cook Time: 10 minutes

Weekend Feasts Unique Recipe Categories with Flexible Plan System

Eggplant Parmesan

Ingredients:
- 1 large eggplant, sliced
- 1/2 cup almond flour
- 1/2 cup marinara sauce (sugar-free)
- 1/2 cup mozzarella cheese, shredded
- 1 tbsp olive oil
- Salt and pepper to taste

Nutritional Information (per serving):
Calories: 310, Protein: 13g, Carbs:12g, Fat: 25g, Fiber: 6g, Sodium: 480mg, Potassium: 630mg

Instructions:
- Preheat oven to 375°F (190°C). Dip eggplant slices in almond flour, season with salt and pepper, and pan-fry in olive oil until golden.
- Layer the eggplant slices in a baking dish, alternating with marinara sauce and mozzarella cheese.
- Bake for 20 minutes until cheese is bubbly and golden.

Servings: 2 **Prep Time:** 15 minutes
Cook Time: 25 minutes

Herb-Crusted Rack of Pork

Ingredients:
- 1 small rack of pork (about 1 lb)
- 1/4 cup almond flour
- 1 tbsp fresh rosemary, chopped
- 1 tbsp fresh thyme, chopped
- 1 tbsp olive oil
- Salt and pepper to taste

Nutritional Information (per serving):
Calories: 460, Protein: 34g, Carbs: 4g, Fat: 34g, Fiber: 2g, Sodium: 300mg, Potassium: 650mg

Instructions:
- Preheat oven to 400°F (200°C). In a small bowl, mix almond flour, rosemary, thyme, and olive oil.
- Rub the pork rack with the herb mixture, and season with salt and pepper.
- Place the pork rack on a baking sheet and roast for 30-35 minutes, or until the internal temperature reaches 145°F (63°C).
- Let the pork rest for 5 minutes before slicing and serving.

Servings: 2 **Prep Time:** 15 minutes
Cook Time: 35 minutes

Roast Chicken with Lemon and Thyme

Ingredients:
- 1 whole chicken (2-3 lbs)
- 2 tbsp olive oil
- 1 lemon, halved
- 2 sprigs fresh thyme
- 4 cloves garlic, minced
- Salt and pepper to taste

Nutritional Information (per serving):
Calories: 450, Protein: 36g, Carbs: 2g, Fat: 32g, Fiber: 1g, Sodium: 390mg, Potassium: 520mg

Instructions:
- Preheat oven to 375°F (190°C). Rub the chicken with olive oil, garlic, salt, and pepper.
- Place the thyme sprigs and lemon halves inside the chicken cavity.
- Roast the chicken in the oven for 45 minutes or until the internal temperature reaches 165°F (74°C).
- Let the chicken rest for 10 minutes before carving

Servings: 2 **Prep Time:** 10 minutes
Cook Time: 45 minutes

Meal-Prep Friendly Recipes   Unique Recipe Categories with Flexible Plan System

Turkey Zucchini Burgers

Ingredients:
- 1 lb ground turkey
- 1 medium zucchini, grated
- 1 clove garlic, minced
- 1 egg
- 1/4 cup almond flour
- Salt and pepper to taste
- 1 tbsp olive oil

Servings: 4 **Prep Time:** 10 minutes
Cook Time: 15 minutes

Instructions:
- In a large bowl, mix ground turkey, grated zucchini, garlic, egg, almond flour, salt, and pepper.
- Form the mixture into 4 patties.
- Heat olive oil in a skillet over medium heat and cook the patties for 5-6 minutes per side, until fully cooked.

Nutritional Information (per serving):
Calories: 250, Protein: 27g, Carbs: 3g, Fat: 14g, Fiber: 1g, Sodium: 220mg, Potassium: 520mg

Cabbage and Sausage Skillet

Ingredients:
- 1/2 lb smoked sausage, sliced
- 1/2 head cabbage, shredded
- 1 onion, chopped
- 2 cloves garlic, minced
- 1 tbsp olive oil
- Salt and pepper to taste

Servings: 4 **Prep Time:** 10 minutes
Cook Time: 20 minutes

Instructions:
- Heat olive oil in a large skillet over medium heat. Add sausage slices and cook until browned.
- Add onion and garlic, and sauté until soft.
- Stir in the shredded cabbage, season with salt and pepper, and cook for 10 minutes until the cabbage is tender.

Nutritional Information (per serving):
Calories: 220, Protein: 10g, Carbs: 6g, Fat: 16g, Fiber: 3g, Sodium: 480mg, Potassium: 400mg

Spinach and Feta Casserole

Ingredients:
- 4 cups fresh spinach, chopped
- 1/2 cup feta cheese, crumbled
- 4 eggs
- 1/4 cup heavy cream
- Salt and pepper to taste
- 1 tbsp olive oil

Servings: 4 **Prep Time:** 10 minutes
Cook Time: 30 minutes

Instructions:
- Preheat oven to 375°F (190°C). In a bowl, mix spinach, feta, eggs, heavy cream, salt, and pepper.
- Grease a baking dish with olive oil and pour the mixture into the dish.
- Bake for 25-30 minutes until set and golden brown on top.

Nutritional Information (per serving):
Calories: 240, Protein: 10g, Carbs: 4g, Fat: 20g, Fiber: 2g, Sodium: 460mg, Potassium: 580mg

Meal-Prep Friendly Recipes Unique Recipe Categories with Flexible Plan System

Baked Salmon with Pesto

Ingredients:
- 2 salmon fillets (4 oz each)
- 2 tbsp homemade or store-bought keto-friendly pesto
- 1 tbsp olive oil
- Salt and pepper to taste

Servings: 2 **Prep Time:** 10 minutes
Cook Time: 20 minutes

Instructions:
- Preheat oven to 375°F (190°C). Rub salmon fillets with olive oil, salt, and pepper.
- Spread pesto evenly over the top of each fillet.
- Bake for 15-20 minutes until the salmon is cooked through.

Nutritional Information (per serving):
Calories: 350, Protein: 287g, Carbs: 2g, Fat: 26g, Fiber: 0g, Sodium: 320mg, Potassium: 580mg

Ground Beef Stuffed Zucchini

Ingredients:
- 4 medium zucchinis, halved lengthwise and scooped
- 1/2 lb ground beef
- 1/2 cup marinara sauce (sugar-free)
- 1/4 cup mozzarella cheese, shredded
- 1 tbsp olive oil
- Salt and pepper to taste

Servings: 4 **Prep Time:** 15 minutes
Cook Time: 20 minutes

Instructions:
- Preheat oven to 375°F (190°C). In a skillet, heat olive oil and brown the ground beef.
- Stir in marinara sauce and season with salt and pepper.
- Fill the zucchini halves with the beef mixture, top with mozzarella, and bake for 20 minutes until the cheese is golden.

Nutritional Information (per serving):
Calories: 260, Protein: 20g, Carbs: 7g, Fat: 18g, Fiber: 2g, Sodium: 470mg, Potassium: 660mg

Egg Muffins with Sausage and Bell Peppers

Ingredients:
- 6 large eggs
- 1/2 cup cooked sausage, crumbled
- 1/2 cup bell peppers, diced
- 1/4 cup cheddar cheese, shredded
- Salt and pepper to taste

Servings: 6 **Prep Time:** 10 minutes
Cook Time: 20 minutes

Instructions:
- Preheat oven to 350°F (175°C). Grease a muffin tin.
- In a bowl, whisk eggs with salt and pepper, then stir in sausage, bell peppers, and cheese.
- Pour the mixture evenly into the muffin cups and bake for 18-20 minutes until set.

Nutritional Information (per serving):
Calories: 180, Protein: 12g, Carbs: 2g, Fat: 14g, Fiber: 0g, Sodium: 320mg, Potassium: 180mg

Meal-Prep Friendly Recipes   Unique Recipe Categories with Flexible Plan System

Chicken and Broccoli Stir-Fry

Ingredients:
- 2 chicken breasts, sliced
- 2 cups broccoli florets
- 1 tbsp soy sauce (or tamari for gluten-free)
- 1 tbsp olive oil
- 2 cloves garlic, minced

Instructions:
- Heat olive oil in a skillet over medium heat. Add sliced chicken and cook until browned.
- Add garlic and broccoli and stir-fry for 8-10 minutes until broccoli is tender. Stir in soy sauce and cook for another minute.

Servings: 2 **Prep Time:** 10 minutes **Cook Time:** 15 minutes

Nutritional Information (per serving):
Calories: 320, Protein: 30g, Carbs: 6g, Fat: 18g, Fiber: 2g, Sodium: 480mg, Potassium: 620mg

Lemon Garlic Baked Cod

Ingredients:
- 2 cod fillets (4 oz each)
- 2 tbsp butter, melted
- 1 clove garlic, minced
- 1 tbsp lemon juice
- Salt and pepper to taste

Instructions:
- Preheat oven to 375°F (190°C). Place cod fillets on a baking sheet and drizzle with melted butter and lemon juice.
- Sprinkle garlic, salt, and pepper on top. Bake for 12-15 minutes until the fish flakes easily with a fork.

Servings: 2 **Prep Time:** 10 minutes **Cook Time:** 15 minutes

Nutritional Information (per serving):
Calories: 210, Protein: 23g, Carbs: 1g, Fat: 12g, Fiber: 0g, Sodium: 290mg, Potassium: 550mg

Chicken Meatballs with Marinara Sauce

Ingredients:
- 1 lb ground chicken
- 1/4 cup Parmesan cheese, grated
- 1 egg
- 1/4 cup almond flour
- 1/2 cup marinara sauce (sugar-free)
- Salt and pepper to taste

Instructions:
- Preheat oven to 375°F (190°C). In a bowl, mix ground chicken, Parmesan, egg, almond flour, salt, and pepper.
- Form mixture into meatballs and place on a baking sheet. Bake for 20 minutes.
- Heat marinara sauce and pour over the meatballs before serving.

Servings: 4 **Prep Time:** 15 minutes **Cook Time:** 25 minutes

Nutritional Information (per serving):
Calories: 260, Protein: 28g, Carbs: 5g, Fat: 14g, Fiber: 2g, Sodium: 460mg, Potassium: 580mg

Keto on a Budget

Unique Recipe Categories with Flexible Plan System

Ground Turkey Stir-Fry with Cabbage

Ingredients:
- 1 lb ground turkey
- 1/2 head of cabbage, shredded
- 1 tbsp olive oil
- 2 cloves garlic, minced
- 1 tbsp soy sauce (or tamari for gluten-free)
- Salt and pepper to taste

Servings: 4 **Prep Time:** 10 minutes **Cook Time:** 15 minutes

Instructions:
- Heat olive oil in a large skillet over medium heat. Add ground turkey and cook until browned, about 7-8 minutes.
- Stir in garlic and shredded cabbage, cook for another 5-6 minutes until the cabbage is tender.
- Add soy sauce, season with salt and pepper, and stir well before serving.

Nutritional Information (per serving):
Calories: 220, Protein: 20g, Carbs: 5g, Fat: 14g, Fiber: 2g, Sodium: 470mg, Potassium: 510mg

Egg Drop Soup

Ingredients:
- 2 cups chicken broth
- 2 eggs, beaten
- 1/4 tsp ginger, minced
- 1 green onion, chopped
- 1 tbsp soy sauce (or tamari for gluten-free)
- Salt and pepper to taste

Servings: 2 **Prep Time:** 5 minutes **Cook Time:** 10 minutes

Instructions:
- Bring the chicken broth to a boil in a pot. Add minced ginger and soy sauce.
- Slowly pour in the beaten eggs while stirring the broth to create thin ribbons of egg.
- Remove from heat, garnish with chopped green onion, and season with salt and pepper.

Nutritional Information (per serving):
Calories: 210, Protein: 10g, Carbs: 2g, Fat: 9g, Fiber: 0g, Sodium: 680mg, Potassium: 310mg

Tuna Salad with Avocado

Ingredients:
- 1 can tuna in water, drained
- 1 avocado, diced
- 2 tbsp mayonnaise
- 1 tsp Dijon mustard
- 1 tbsp lemon juice
- Salt and pepper to taste

Servings: 2 **Prep Time:** 10 minutes

Instructions:
- In a bowl, combine drained tuna, diced avocado, mayonnaise, Dijon mustard, and lemon juice.
- Stir well and season with salt and pepper to taste. Serve on lettuce leaves or eat as is.

Nutritional Information (per serving):
Calories: 320, Protein: 22g, Carbs: 5g, Fat: 24g, Fiber: 4g, Sodium: 320mg, Potassium: 620mg

Keto for Families Unique Recipe Categories with Flexible Plan System

Chicken Alfredo Bake

Ingredients:
- 2 chicken breasts, cooked and shredded
- 2 cups zucchini noodles (zoodles)
- 1/2 cup heavy cream
- 1/2 cup Parmesan cheese, grated
- 1/2 cup mozzarella cheese, shredded
- 1 clove garlic, minced
- Salt and pepper to taste

Servings: 4 **Prep Time:** 10 minutes
Cook Time: 25 minutes

Instructions:
- Preheat oven to 375°F (190°C). In a bowl, mix shredded chicken, zucchini noodles, heavy cream, Parmesan, garlic, salt, and pepper.
- Pour the mixture into a baking dish and top with shredded mozzarella.
- Bake for 20-25 minutes until the cheese is melted and bubbly.

Nutritional Information (per serving):
Calories: 350, Protein: 28g, Carbs: 4g, Fat: 24g, Fiber: 1g, Sodium: 420mg, Potassium: 580mg

BBQ Chicken Thighs

Ingredients:
- 4 chicken thighs
- 1/4 cup sugar-free BBQ sauce
- 1 tbsp olive oil
- Salt and pepper to taste

Servings: 4 **Prep Time:** 5 minutes
Cook Time: 30 minutes

Instructions:
- Preheat oven to 375°F (190°C). Brush chicken thighs with olive oil and season with salt and pepper.
- Place the thighs on a baking sheet and bake for 25 minutes.
- Brush each thigh with BBQ sauce and bake for another 5 minutes.

Nutritional Information (per serving):
Calories: 320, Protein: 25g, Carbs: 3g, Fat: 23g, Fiber: 0g, Sodium: 360mg, Potassium: 450mg

Meatloaf with Hidden Vegetables

Ingredients:
- 1 lb ground beef
- 1/2 cup zucchini, finely grated
- 1/2 cup carrots, finely grated
- 1/4 cup almond flour
- 1 egg
- 1/4 cup sugar-free ketchup
- Salt and pepper to taste

Servings: 4 **Prep Time:** 15 minutes
Cook Time: 45 minutes

Instructions:
- Preheat oven to 375°F (190°C). In a bowl, mix ground beef, zucchini, carrots, almond flour, egg, salt, and pepper.
- Press the mixture into a loaf pan and spread the ketchup on top.
- Bake for 45 minutes or until the meatloaf is fully cooked.

Nutritional Information (per serving):
Calories: 350, Protein: 28g, Carbs: 6g, Fat: 24g, Fiber: 2g, Sodium: 420mg, Potassium: 640mg

International Keto Recipes Unique Recipe Categories with Flexible Plan System

Chicken Tikka Masala

Ingredients:
- 2 chicken breasts, cubed
- 1/2 cup heavy cream
- 1/2 cup plain yogurt (unsweetened, full-fat)
- 1 tbsp tomato paste
- 1 tbsp garam masala
- 1 tsp turmeric
- 1 tsp cumin
- 2 cloves garlic, minced
- 1 tbsp olive oil
- Salt and pepper to taste

Servings: 4 **Prep Time:** 10 minutes **Cook Time:** 25 minutes

Instructions:
- Heat olive oil in a skillet over medium heat. Add cubed chicken and season with garam masala, turmeric, and cumin. Cook until browned, about 7-8 minutes.
- Stir in garlic, tomato paste, and yogurt, cooking for another 2 minutes.
- Add heavy cream, lower heat, and simmer for 15 minutes until the sauce thickens.

Nutritional Information (per serving):
Calories: 370, Protein: 30g, Carbs: 5g, Fat: 25g, Fiber: 1g, Sodium: 420mg, Potassium: 640mg

Thai Green Curry with Shrimp

Ingredients:
- 1 lb shrimp, peeled and deveined
- 1/2 cup coconut milk (full-fat)
- 2 tbsp green curry paste (check for keto-friendly options)
- 1 red bell pepper, sliced
- 1 zucchini, sliced
- 1 tbsp olive oil
- 1/4 cup fresh cilantro, chopped
- 1 lime, quartered for garnish
- Salt and pepper to taste

Servings: 4 **Prep Time:** 10 minutes **Cook Time:** 20 minutes

Instructions:
- Heat olive oil in a skillet over medium heat. Add green curry paste and sauté for 1 minute until fragrant.
- Stir in coconut milk, bell pepper, and zucchini. Simmer for 10 minutes until the vegetables are tender.
- Add shrimp and cook for another 5 minutes until the shrimp are opaque. Garnish with cilantro and lime wedges before serving.

Nutritional Information (per serving):
Calories: 300, Protein: 25g, Carbs: 7g, Fat: 18g, Fiber: 2g, Sodium: 550mg, Potassium: 480mg

Mexican Enchilada Casserole

Ingredients:
- 1 lb ground beef
- 1/2 cup enchilada sauce (sugar-free)
- 1/2 cup shredded cheddar cheese
- 1/4 cup sour cream
- 1/2 cup diced tomatoes
- 1/4 cup black olives, sliced
- 1 tbsp olive oil
- Salt and pepper to taste

Nutritional Information (per serving):
Calories: 400, Protein: 28g, Carbs: 8g, Fat: 30g, Fiber: 3g, Sodium: 640mg, Potassium: 540mg

Instructions:
- Preheat oven to 375°F (190°C). Heat olive oil in a skillet and brown ground beef, seasoning with salt and pepper.
- Stir in enchilada sauce and tomatoes, and cook for 5 minutes.
- Pour the mixture into a baking dish, top with shredded cheese, and bake for 15-20 minutes until cheese is melted and bubbly. Garnish with sour cream and black olives before serving.

Servings: 4 **Prep Time:** 15 minutes **Cook Time:** 25 minutes

Bonus Recipe for Thanksgiving

Herb-Roasted Turkey with Cauliflower Mash

Ingredients:
For the Turkey:
- 1 whole turkey (10-12 lbs)
- 1/4 cup olive oil or melted butter
- 4 cloves garlic, minced
- 2 tbsp fresh rosemary, chopped
- 2 tbsp fresh thyme, chopped
- 1 tbsp fresh sage, chopped
- Salt and pepper to taste
- 1 lemon, halved
- 1 onion, quartered
- 2 cups chicken broth

For the Cauliflower Mash:
- 1 large head of cauliflower, cut into florets
- 1/4 cup heavy cream
- 2 tbsp butter
- 1/2 cup shredded Parmesan cheese
- Salt and pepper to taste
- Fresh parsley for garnish

Prep. time: 30 min | Cooking time: 2-3 hours (depending on the size of the turkey) | Servings: 8

Instructions:
Prepare the Turkey:
- Preheat the oven to 350°F (175°C).
- In a small bowl, combine olive oil (or melted butter), garlic, rosemary, thyme, sage, salt, and pepper.
- Pat the turkey dry and rub the herb mixture generously over the entire turkey, including under the skin.
- Stuff the cavity with lemon halves and onion quarters.
- Place the turkey on a rack in a roasting pan. Pour the chicken broth into the bottom of the pan.
- Roast the turkey, basting occasionally with the pan juices, until it reaches an internal temperature of 165°F (74°C) in the thickest part of the thigh. This typically takes 2-3 hours, depending on the size of the turkey.
- Let the turkey rest for 20-30 minutes before carving.

Make the Cauliflower Mash:
- While the turkey is roasting, steam or boil the cauliflower florets until they are fork-tender (about 10-12 minutes).
- Drain and transfer the cauliflower to a food processor. Add heavy cream, butter, and Parmesan cheese. Process until smooth and creamy.
- Season with salt and pepper to taste, and garnish with fresh parsley before serving.

Nutritional Information (Per Serving): • Calories: 490 • Protein: 65g • Carbohydrates: 6g • Fats: 23g • Fiber: 3g • Cholesterol: 190mg • Sodium: 600mg • Potassium: 800mg

Bonus Recipe for Thanksgiving

Keto Thanksgiving Stuffing

Ingredients:
- 1 lb ground sausage
- 1/2 cup celery, chopped
- 1/2 cup onion, chopped
- 1 cup mushrooms, sliced
- 1/2 cup chicken broth
- 1/4 cup almond flour
- 2 tbsp fresh sage, chopped
- 1 tbsp fresh thyme, chopped
- Salt and pepper to taste

Prep. time: 30 min | Cooking time: 2-3 hours (depending on the size of the turkey) | Servings: 8

Instructions:
- Preheat oven to 350°F (175°C).
- In a large skillet, cook sausage over medium heat until browned. Remove and set aside.
- In the same skillet, sauté celery, onion, and mushrooms until tender.
- Add sausage back to the skillet. Stir in chicken broth, almond flour, sage, thyme, salt, and pepper.
- Transfer the mixture to a baking dish.
- Bake for 25-30 minutes, until the top is golden and crispy.

Nutritional Information (Per Serving): • Calories: 250 • Protein: 12g • Carbohydrates: 5g • Fats: 20g • Fiber: 2g

A delicious low-carb alternative to traditional stuffing, packed with flavor and perfect for Thanksgiving.

Bonus Recipe for Christmas

Holiday Ham with Cranberry Glaze

Ingredients:

For the Ham:
- 1 (8-10 lb) fully cooked bone-in ham
- Whole cloves (optional, for studding the ham)
- 1/2 cup water (for roasting pan)

For the Cranberry Glaze:
- 1 cup fresh or frozen cranberries
- 1/4 cup sugar-free maple syrup
- 1/4 cup powdered erythritol or monk fruit sweetener
- 1/4 cup apple cider vinegar
- 2 tbsp Dijon mustard
- 1 tsp orange zest (optional)
- 1/2 tsp ground cinnamon
- 1/4 tsp ground cloves
- 1/4 cup water (for sauce)

Prep. time: 30 min | Cooking time: 2-3 hours (depending on the size of the turkey) | Servings: 8

Instructions:

Prepare the Ham:
- Preheat the oven to 325°F (160°C).
- If desired, use a sharp knife to score the surface of the ham in a diamond pattern, about 1/4 inch deep. Optionally, stud the ham with whole cloves in the center of each diamond for added flavor.
- Place the ham, cut side down, in a roasting pan and add 1/2 cup of water to the bottom of the pan to prevent drying. Cover the ham loosely with aluminum foil.

Bake the Ham:
- Bake the ham for 1.5 to 2 hours, or until the internal temperature reaches 140°F (60°C). Baste the ham with its juices halfway through cooking.

Prepare the Cranberry Glaze:
- While the ham is baking, combine cranberries, sugar-free maple syrup, erythritol, apple cider vinegar, Dijon mustard, orange zest, cinnamon, ground cloves, and 1/4 cup water in a medium saucepan.
- Bring the mixture to a simmer over medium heat, stirring occasionally. Cook until the cranberries burst and the sauce thickens, about 8-10 minutes.
- Use an immersion blender or transfer to a regular blender to blend until smooth. Set aside.

Glaze the Ham:
- After the ham has reached 140°F (60°C), remove it from the oven and increase the oven temperature to 425°F (220°C).
- Generously brush the cranberry glaze over the entire surface of the ham.
- Return the ham to the oven, uncovered, for an additional 15-20 minutes, or until the glaze becomes caramelized and sticky. Keep an eye on it to avoid burning.

Rest and Serve:
- Remove the ham from the oven and let it rest for 10-15 minutes before carving.
- Serve with extra cranberry glaze on the side.

This Keto-friendly holiday ham is sweetened with sugar-free syrup and erythritol, making it a perfect centerpiece for any holiday table while keeping it low-carb. The tangy cranberry glaze adds a festive touch, balancing sweet and savory flavors.

Nutritional Information (Per Serving): • Calories: 320 • Protein: 30g • Carbohydrates: 4g • Fats: 20g • Fiber: 1g • Cholesterol: 85mg • Sodium: 1200mg • Potassium: 500mg

Bonus Recipe for Christmas

Pecan Pie Bars

Ingredients:
For the Crust:
- 2 cups almond flour
- 1/4 cup coconut flour
- 1/4 cup powdered erythritol or monk fruit sweetener
- 1/2 cup butter, melted
- Pinch of salt

For the Pecan Filling:
- 1 cup pecans, roughly chopped
- 1/2 cup butter
- 1/2 cup sugar-free maple syrup
- 1/3 cup powdered erythritol or monk fruit sweetener
- 1 tsp vanilla extract
- 2 large eggs, beaten

Servings: 16 bars | Prep Time: 15 minutes | Cook Time: 35-40 minutes

Instructions:

Prepare the Crust:
- Preheat the oven to 350°F (175°C) and line an 8x8 inch baking pan with parchment paper.
- In a mixing bowl, combine almond flour, coconut flour, erythritol, and melted butter. Stir until a dough forms.
- Press the dough evenly into the bottom of the prepared baking pan. Bake for 10-12 minutes until the edges are lightly golden. Remove from the oven and set aside.

Prepare the Pecan Filling:
- In a saucepan over medium heat, melt the butter, sugar-free syrup, and erythritol together. Stir until fully combined and slightly thickened (about 5 minutes).
- Remove the saucepan from heat and stir in vanilla extract and beaten eggs. Mix quickly to avoid scrambling the eggs.
- Add the chopped pecans and stir until well-coated.

Assemble the Bars:
- Pour the pecan filling over the pre-baked crust and spread evenly.
- Bake for an additional 20-25 minutes until the filling is set and golden.
- Allow the bars to cool completely before cutting into squares.

Nutritional Information (Per Serving): • Calories: 220 • Protein: 4g • Carbohydrates: 4g • Fats: 22g • Fiber: 3g • Cholesterol: 50mg • Sodium: 150mg • Potassium: 80m

A low-carb version of a holiday favorite with a buttery almond flour crust and a rich pecan filling

Week-by-Week Flexible Meal Plan and Customization Guide

Embarking on a keto diet can be exciting, but sticking to it requires planning and preparation. To make the process easier and more manageable, this week-by-week meal plan provides a structured guide with **breakfast, lunch, dinner, and snack** options. You can follow the plan as is, or mix and match recipes based on your preferences and availability of ingredients.

At the end of the 30 days, you'll have developed a strong foundation for your keto journey, understanding how to maintain ketosis while enjoying a variety of flavorful meals.

Week 1: Simple Keto Recipes to Get You Started

	Breakfast	Lunch	Dinner	Snack
Day 1	Pancakes with Butter and Syrup, 10	Chicken Caesar Salad with Avocado, 21	Garlic Butter Shrimp with Zoodles, 32	Deviled Eggs with Bacon, 43
Day 2	Avocado and Bacon Omelette, 10	Zucchini Noodles with Pesto and Grilled Chicken, 21	Beef Stroganoff, 40	Parmesan Crisps with Herbs, 43
Day 3	Chia Seed Pudding with Almonds, 11	Tuna Salad Lettuce Wraps, 22	Baked Salmon with Lemon and Asparagus, 33	Avocado and Tuna Salad Cups, 44
Day 4	Coconut Flour Waffles with Berries, 11	Cobb Salad with Blue Cheese Dressing, 22	Keto-Friendly Lasagna with Zucchini Noodles, 33	Cheese-Stuffed Mushrooms, 44
Day 5	Spinach and Cheese Frittata, 12	Bacon-Wrapped Chicken Tenders, 23	Grilled Chicken with Avocado Salsa, 34	Baked Avocado Fries, 46
Day 6	Smoothie Bowl with Nuts and Seeds, 12	Shrimp and Avocado Salad, 23	Pork Chops with Creamy Mushroom Sauce, 34	Bacon-Wrapped Jalapeño Poppers, 46
Day 7	Sausage and Egg Muffins, 13	Broccoli and Cheddar Soup, 24	Shepherd's Pie with Cauliflower Mash, 35	Spinach Artichoke Dip with Veggies, 47

Week 1

Weekly Overview

Goal for Week 1: Begin the transition into ketosis by gradually reducing carb intake and increasing healthy fats. This helps reduce the likelihood of Keto flu symptoms.

Focus: Start with simple, approachable meals to ease into the Keto lifestyle without feeling overwhelmed. This week emphasizes flavor and familiar ingredients to make the transition enjoyable.

Customization Tips

Swap Ingredients: If a recipe calls for a specific protein (like chicken or beef), feel free to substitute with other Keto-friendly proteins, such as turkey or fish, to keep meals varied.

Meal Size Adjustments: If you're hungry, increase the fat portion by adding avocado, cheese, or nuts. Conversely, reduce portions if you feel overly full.

Spice It Up: Use a variety of herbs and spices (like garlic, basil, and paprika) to enhance flavors without adding carbs.

Meal Prep and Shopping Tips

Batch Cooking: For breakfasts, consider preparing a large batch of Keto Pancakes or Sausage and Egg Muffins on Sunday. Store them in the fridge for easy grab-and-go meals throughout the week.

Storage Tips: Keep fresh vegetables like spinach and avocado on hand, and use airtight containers to store meal preps for several days to keep ingredients fresh.

Shopping Tip: Buy larger portions of ingredients like eggs, avocado, and leafy greens. These versatile staples are used in many recipes throughout the week.

Electrolyte Balance

Stay Hydrated: Keto diets can initially cause water loss, so drink plenty of water daily.

Add Sodium: Salt your meals more generously than usual, or consider sipping on bone broth to maintain sodium levels.

Potassium-Rich Foods: Leafy greens like spinach and avocado are high in potassium, which can help maintain energy levels and reduce muscle cramps.

Weekly Goal and Encouragement

Aim to feel more energy-stable and experience fewer carb cravings by the end of the week. Be patient as your body adjusts.

Celebrate small wins each day —whether it's resisting a carb craving, trying a new recipe, or simply feeling more energized. Remind yourself that this is the beginning of a health transformation!

Shopping List by Food Group for Week 1

Proteins
Chicken breast
Bacon
Beef (for stir-fry and shepherd's pie)
Salmon fillet
Pork chops
Sausage
Canned tuna
Eggs
Shrimp

Vegetables
Romaine lettuce
Zucchini (for noodles)
Broccoli
Asparagus
Spinach
Mushrooms
Cauliflower
Jalapenos
Avocado
Tomato
Onion
Celery
Artichoke hearts

Fruits (Low-Carb)
Mixed berries (for waffles and smoothie bowls)
Lemon (for dressings and marinades)
Lime (for avocado salsa)

Pantry Essentials
Almond flour
Coconut flour
Chia seeds
Baking powder
Keto-friendly syrup
Mayonnaise
Caesar dressing
Blue cheese dressing
Marinara sauce (sugar-free)
Soy sauce or tamari
Italian herbs
Stevia or preferred sweetener

Dairy and Fats
Butter
Heavy cream
Cheese (Parmesan, blue cheese, cheddar, mozzarella)
Cream cheese
Almond butter
Coconut oil
Olive oil

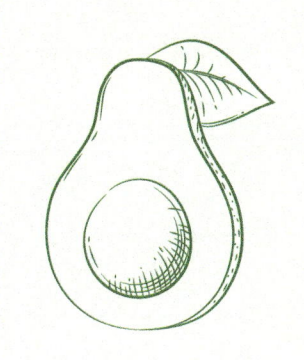

Week 2: Exploring New Flavors and Ingredients

This week, we're focusing on exploring new flavors and ingredients to keep your Keto journey exciting. By incorporating a greater variety of recipes, you'll be able to experiment with flavors, textures, and nutritional benefits while deepening your understanding of what works best for you on the Keto diet.

	Breakfast	**Lunch**	**Dinner**	**Snack**
Day 1	French Toast with Cinnamon, 13	Grilled Steak Salad with Balsamic Vinaigrette, 25	Lamb Chops with Garlic and Herbs, 35	Coconut Macaroons, 47
Day 2	Bulletproof Coffee, 14	Caprese Stuffed Avocados, 25	Cauliflower Crust Pizza with Pepperoni, 36	Zucchini Chips with Ranch Dip, 48
Day 3	Zucchini and Cheese Hash Browns, 14	Chili with Sour Cream, 26	Chicken Alfredo with Broccoli, 36	Prosciutto-Wrapped Asparagus, 48
Day 4	Breakfast Burrito with Sausage, 15	Egg Salad on Keto Bread, 26	Stuffed Bell Peppers with Ground Beef, 37	Garlic Knots, 49
Day 5	Smoked Salmon and Cream Cheese Roll-Ups, 15	BLT Salad, 27	Meatloaf with Green Beans, 37	Chocolate Almond Fat Bombs, 50
Day 6	Asparagus and Ham Quiche, 16	Cauliflower Fried Rice with Pork, 27	Keto-Friendly Chicken Parmesan, 38	Cheese and Olive Skewers, 50
Day 7	Almond Flour Muffins with Blueberries, 16	Turkey and Cheese Roll-Ups, 28	Seared Scallops with Garlic Butter, 38	Guacamole with Pork Rinds, 51

You're building momentum and variety on Keto — great work! Keep enjoying new flavors and focusing on how these meals make you feel. Remember, every meal is an opportunity to fuel your journey and reinforce your commitment to health and wellness.

Week 2

Weekly Overview

This week introduces more variety to your keto meal plan, offering exciting dishes that keep your meals interesting while maintaining the core principles of the ketogenic diet.

With recipes designed to enhance your nutritional intake and satisfaction, you'll be enjoying everything from classic comfort foods to vibrant, fresh salads and creative snacks.

This variety will help ensure that the keto diet remains enjoyable, sustainable, and delicious.

Customization Tips:

Protein Swaps: Feel free to substitute proteins based on preference or availability. For example, use shrimp instead of chicken in salads or ground turkey instead of ground beef.

Flavor Enhancements: Add fresh herbs like dill, cilantro, or basil to enhance the flavors of salads and seafood dishes.

Portion Adjustments: Adjust portion sizes to meet your hunger levels or caloric needs; for instance, double the salad for a heartier meal or reduce portions if you feel satisfied with less.

Meal Prep Tips:

Batch Cooking: Prepare several servings of Zucchini Chips, Guacamole, and Egg Salad to use throughout the week, making snack time quicker and easier.

Ingredient Pre-Prep: Dice vegetables like tomatoes, bell peppers, and lettuce, and store them in airtight containers to save prep time during the week. You can also pre-cook bacon and store it for recipes like Turkey Club Wraps and Breakfast Frittatas.

Electrolyte and Health Tips:

Hydration: Keep hydrated by drinking plenty of water and adding electrolyte-rich options like bone broth or coconut water. This is especially helpful as you increase your activity levels with a diet high in whole foods.

Electrolytes: Add avocado, nuts, and leafy greens into your meals to help maintain electrolyte balance. Consider adding a sprinkle of pink *Himalayan salt* for sodium and magnesium content.

Shopping List by Food Group for Week 2

Proteins
Steak
Lamb chops
Ground beef (for chili and meatloaf)
Chicken breast
Sausage
Smoked salmon
Bacon
Turkey breast slices
Prosciutto
Ground pork
Scallops

Vegetables
Romaine lettuce
Cherry tomatoes
Cucumber
Zucchini
Bell peppers
Avocado
Broccoli
Asparagus
Green beans
Cauliflower (for crust and fried rice)
Spinach (for muffins)
Fresh basil, parsley, and dill

Eggs and Dairy
Eggs
Grass-fed butter
Heavy cream
Parmesan cheese
Shredded mozzarella cheese
Cream cheese
Cheese cubes and slices
Almond flour (for quiche, garlic knots, muffins)

Oils and Fats
Olive oil
Coconut oil
MCT oil (for Bulletproof coffee)
Almond butter (for fat bombs)
Sesame oil

Additional Pantry Items
Unsweetened shredded coconut (for macaroons)
Keto-friendly sweetener (for fat bombs, muffins)
Marinara sauce
Keto bread
Low-carb tortillas
Pork rinds

Herbs, Spices, and Flavorings
Garlic powder
Italian seasoning
Chili powder
Cumin
Salt and pepper
Ranch seasoning (for dip)
Vanilla extract
Cinnamon
Balsamic vinegar

Fruits
Blueberries
Lime (for guacamole)

Week 3. Energizing and Nutritious Meals

As you settle into your keto routine, Week 3 is all about fueling your body with energizing, nutrient-dense meals. By now, you'll be feeling more energized and confident in your keto cooking skills. The meals this week are designed to provide sustained energy, keep cravings in check, and keep you feeling satisfied as your body adapts to burning fat for fuel.

	Breakfast	Lunch	Dinner	Snack
Day 1	Mushroom and Swiss Scramble, 17	Salmon Salad with Lemon Dill Dressing, 28	Tacos with Lettuce Wraps, 41	Cauliflower Bites with Buffalo Sauce, 51
Day 2	Breakfast Casserole with Bacon, 17	Chicken Salad with Pecans, 29	Zucchini Lasagna with Ricotta, 39	Chocolate Bark with Nuts, 52
Day 3	Granola with Coconut and Pecans, 18	Beef Taco Salad with Avocado, 29	Beef Stroganoff, 40	Coconut Macaroons, 47
Day 4	Egg and Avocado Toast (using Keto bread), 18	Spinach and Feta Stuffed Chicken, 30	Grilled Lemon Herb Chicken Thighs, 40	Buffalo Chicken Dip, 49
Day 5	Crepes with Cream Cheese Filling, 19	Meatballs with Marinara Sauce, 30	Chicken Pot Pie, 41	Guacamole with Pork Rinds, 51
Day 6	Cheddar and Herb Biscuits, 19	Turkey Club Wraps, 24	Baked Salmon with Pesto, 71	Baked Avocado Fries, 46
Day 7	Spinach and Cheese Frittata, 12	BLT Salad, 27	Pork Chops with Creamy Mushroom Sauce, 34	Zucchini Chips with Ranch Dip, 48

Keep going strong — by Week 3, you're creating sustainable Keto habits that fuel your body and mind. Embrace the benefits and remind yourself of the progress you've made. This is your week to solidify routines that will support you for the long term!